HIDDEN LORE
™

Second Edition Screen and Lore

By Allen Varney, Brian Campbell, Phil Brucato and John R. Robey

Credits

Written by: *Rotes/ Mages:* Allen Varney; *Setting:* John R. Robey, Brian Campbell; *Mages/ St. Hints:* Phil Brucato; *Sphere sheets:* Designed by Wayne Peacock; *Spheres:* Kevin A. Murphey, Phil Brucato; *Fiction:* Deena McKinney

Developed by: Phil Brucato

Edited by: Cynthia Summers

Vice President in Charge of Production: Richard Thomas

Art Directors: Lawrence Snelly & Aileen E. Miles

Layout and Typesetting: Aileen E. Miles

Art: John Cobb, Daryll Elliott, Scott Johnson, Dan Smith, Andrew Trabbald, Lawrence Allen Williams

Maps: John Park

Back Cover Art: Alex Shiekman

Front Cover Art: Mark Jackson

Front and Back Cover Design: Kathleen Ryan & Aileen E. Miles

SUITE 100
780 PARK NORTH BLVD.
CLARKSTON, GA 30021

Special Thanks to:

Brad "Conan" **Butkovich**, for spreading NERO's gospel throughout the land.

Wes "Not My Fault" **Harris**, for joining Mark in Quakesville.

Mike "Wolfdaddy" **Krause**, for raising his child among the pack.

Danny "Outta Here" **Landers**, for taking his toys and going back to school.

Elizabeth "Karate Kid III" **McKee**, for her dancing exploits at DragonCon.

Christian "The Great Grape Ape" **Naberhaus**, for his dietary experiment at the company picnic.

Stephe "Jet Set" **Pagel**, for letting his rent money go to waste.

Jane "Reach Out and Kill Someone" **Palmer**, for the Furious Phone-Line Follies.

Fred "Collectible Tarot Card" **Yelk**, for dodging the **Mage** developer's thrown pillows.

Diane "Cattleprod" **Zamojski**, for threatening to liven up the party the hard way.

Sarah "Mystery Mistress" **Timbrook**, for having an amazingly useful shadow.

Nathan "Invisible" **Jones**, for being Sarah's amazingly useful shadow.

Rachel (Remy) "Fast Talker" **Blaine**, for *something* — if only we could only understand what she just said…

Greg "Knockers" **Fountain**, for discovering just how silly a $12.00 Halloween gargoyle can be.

A Parting Howl

Yipe! It seems like just yesterday that a handful of wolves fought it out for space in an old office building. Now we've moved to a new headquarters and our staff has boomed proportionately. To be honest, I kinda miss the days when our pack of black-leather degenerates would grumble off to Steak and Ale, scare the crap out of the wait staff, stake out our own room and complain endlessly about how little money we were paid for the work we did. We're still not rich, but our respectability quotient has gone up a bit since then (sigh).

Sadly, two of our longtime packmates have departed for other forests. Bill Bridges, **Werewolf's** developer and co-creator, has joined HDI (Andrew Greenberg's computer game company), while convention god Danny Landers has returned to school to pursue his masters degree. Their jobs have fallen into the capable hands of Ethan Skemp (formerly Game Studio Editor) and Kim Pullen, respectively. No one, however, can match the contributions these two have made during their stay here. We'll miss them both.

Good luck, guys.

HIDDEN LORE ™

Contents

Introduction

The old woman gave Cat a haughty sniff as the young mage blew a loud, smacking bubble.

"What do you mean, I have to go wash my hands?" Cat asked. "What kinda screwy library is this, anyway?"

The woman slapped a ruler down hard on her desk. Cat jumped.

"This, young lady, is a place where the tomes of accumulated knowledge from many Houses and many ages past have been gathered for the benefit of those who wish to learn and better themselves. Yet, I find it hard to believe that someone who has obviously slept in her clothes without the benefit of regular baths would even be interested." *She straightened her bun, which had come loose.*

"Who the hell died and made you health inspector of the universe?" Cat snarled.

The librarian's shaky old fingers lowered her glasses as she peered over them with a withering look.

"Here, young lady, I am not just the health inspector of the universe, I am the universe. If you wish to paw my books, you'll wash those grimy mitts now!"

How To Use This Book

Let's be honest: this is an overflow book. The material here had to be cut from **Mage Second Edition** to bring the book down to an affordable size. The goodies herein, however, were too good to go to waste. While they aren't essential to playing the game, they're nice tidbits to have around.

A quick overview of this book's contents: a pile of rotes and Effects for your players and Storyteller characters; some lesser-known facts about the mystick world, including a short Who's Who; quick-reference Sphere sheets; a setting Chantry based in Seattle; variant game suggestions and more. The general organization is as follows: **Chapter One** is general stuff for players, **Chapter Two** concerns the Conjurer's Cubbyhole, a magic shop that is more than it appears. **Chapter Three**'s information is best left in Storyteller hands, and **Chapter Four** offers a selection of photocopiable handouts for all **Mage** players.

Open, peruse and enjoy.

Chapter One: Lore

"98, 99, 100...." Broty sheepishly opened his eyes, feeling like a kid playing hide-and-go-seek. He paused before pulling back the crimson tapestries.

Gone was the Provincial bedroom of the Chantry. Instead, Broty sat on the edge of a divan in a brilliantly tiled room. Pots of giant blood-red tulips sat about a tinkling fountain, and heady incense burned his eyes. From somewhere outside the room, he heard drums and the jangle of bells. Opening the carved and painted door, he gazed dumbly out into a garden of sinful delights: semi-naked dancers, hookahs, platters of honeyed delicacies and towering ferns that hid flesh but not sounds. As the young mage gaped, an houri swirled by Broty with a silver tray laden with sweetmeats.

"Bonbon?" she asked with a promising smile.

The following sections give both players and Storytellers some new things to play with — new magicks, possible game variations, suggestions for "personalizing" a mage beyond the simple statistics and a collection of famous (and infamous) Ascension Warriors.

Chronicle Suggestions

Why stay limited to the obvious? While the **Mage** rulebook provides the framework for a basic game, the suggestions in this section might add some spice to your troupe's chronicle.

Alternative Gaming Styles

A **Mage** game need not revolve around one Storyteller and a group of one-character players. The following variations might add some spice to your chronicle, and help you to avoid Storyteller (or player) burnout.

• One-on-One

Player preludes do not have to be the only occasions in which a Storyteller and player go at it alone. The most common mythical stories of heroism are based on the idea of a hero traveling alone. That one person struggles against everything the world can throw at him. He journeys into darkness and emerges with a greater knowledge of himself and the world around him.

Mage, more than any other roleplaying game, lends itself well to single-player sessions. Quiets, Seekings, solo quests, romantic interludes, family crises, brushes with the law and imprisonment in a Paradox Realm are just a few of the possibilities if only one player is available for a game. Such interludes work better if they fit into a larger storyline, but with a quick wit and an imaginative player, really powerful games can spring from an otherwise wasted evening.

It's generally best to throw the dice out entirely during such sessions, or to use them only for the occasional Willpower roll. The real strengths of one-on-one stories come from the imagination invested and the power of the situations involved. A strong grasp of the background characters, their motivations and their relationships to your player's character are essential. Who are these people? What do they want? What will they do to get it? If your player has some empathy for her mage, you can get some real chemistry going.

Think up an intriguing situation, one where something important is on the line. Is the main character's lover having an affair? Is the cabal's detective ally suspicious of a mage's shady past? Is the mage at odds with her Avatar, or is she questing for further levels of Arete? Has she lost Willpower, and thus the power to work magick the way she used to? Did someone kidnap her dog and sell it to a lab for experiments? A one-on-one storyline should carry high emotional stakes for the player as well as her character. Run well, such a game can be a memorable chronicle chapter.

• Troupe Play

It's also possible for each player to have a "stable" of characters. In full troupe play, everyone has access to a wide variety of options. Each player might have one powerful mage, one or two acolytes and maybe even one or two "mundane" characters. In each chapter, or each story, the players decide who will play the mages, the acolytes and the mundanes. Then you can shift focus among them. One session might involve the Celestial Chorus mage tending to her flock with assistance from the acolytes, while the next might feature an Akashic Brother breaking into a corporation headquarters while trying to keep his magickal nature secret from the two private investigators helping him. As long as you occasionally run a session in which all the main characters can work together, this approach solves the problem of trying to integrate vastly different characters.

• Troupe Storytelling

If the troupe always relies on the same Storyteller, it can wear that person out. With troupe Storytelling, certain players take turns running the game. They might choose to switch every few weeks, or for each story, each chapter (through a series of cliffhangers) or even in the middle of a session. Another approach is to divide areas geographically. One player is responsible for the city, one has developed a plot in the wilderness, the third has constructed a few Otherworld plots, and the fourth may specialize in the realms of the Restless Dead. As long as the characters serve as the common ground, it's a great way to prevent Storyteller burn-out.

• Blue-Booking

Christened by game designer Aaron Allston, this variation on one-on-one gaming allows one or two players to write stories about the characters' affairs between game sessions. These "blue books" (named for college exam booklets) make excellent resources for backgrounds, plot threads, Storyteller characters and narrative elements (foreshadowing, flashbacks, etc.), and help both players and Storytellers flesh their mages out.

Blue-booking sessions can run either as written exchanges, passing the book back and forth, or as single-writer projects which players hand in to you. Players need not be Mercedes Lackey to turn in a good blue book; imagination and empathy are more important than style. Especially good stories might be worth an extra experience point, based on the effort involved. This should not be abused, however. A blue book story ought to explore some new details in the character's life — his private habits, past relationships, personality quirks, obsessions, etc. A string of "I met a Technomancer and killed him" vignettes would be a cheap appeal for power-gaming, and deserves to be ignored. We recommend that only one to two blue-booking sessions be "played" between each group game; otherwise, the writers among the troupe quickly advance over the other players. Used wisely, however, blue-book stories can add immeasurably to a chronicle's depth and texture.

Miniatures

Although it's not really a combat-oriented game, a **Mage** chronicle which uses 25mm miniatures gains some extra dimensions: clarity ("Where's that HIT Mark? Can he see me yet?"), excitement ("There's only 15 feet between me and that waterfall! Help!"), atmosphere ("Yipe! *That* just walked in?") and a sense of focus. After all, a game with obvious pieces and a gameboard keeps people from becoming distracted by bowls of munchies or nearby Significant Others.

Several figure lines represent **Mage's** archaic-tech diversity well. Ral Partha has an extensive selection of **Mage**, **Werewolf** and **Vampire** figures available; their *Shadowrun* figures also work well. Leading Edge's *Terminator II* collection adds some good HIT Marks to the mix, and RAFM's *Call of Cthulhu* minis suit archaic scenarios. Troupes may choose to paint (or not to paint, as it were) their figures to suit the game's flavor and the players' preferences. 1" hex maps, especially the roll-up vinyl variety, make ideal gameboards — so long as you use water-based pens to draw out your setting! Ambitious Storytellers might even use model railroad kits to represent buildings and landscapes. Any and all of these props can be found in any good game or hobby store.

Rules

The rules for utilizing miniatures are pretty simple:

• Each 1" hex represents one yard for the purposes of movement or range (see "Taking Actions" in Chapter Ten for movement rates and "Combat" for weapon ranges). The average person can walk seven yards, jog 14 and run 26, which translates to 7", 14" or 26" per turn. High Dexterity characters can move even faster. Moving and acting in the same turn requires splitting your Dice Pool.

• The direction of the hex indicates which way the character is facing, and he, she or it generally has a triangular field of vision going out from there. Under most circumstances, objects in between figures block vision and fire, although magick may modify this. A character may only attack someone she's facing or otherwise able to see.

• A walking or jogging character may change her facing by one "side" for each hex she moves. If she runs, she can only change facing once for every hex she moves. She may only move one way (i.e., all running or all walking) per turn. If she chooses to go backwards, she can only move 4" per turn, period.

• Characters must be within a hex of each other to touch or fight unless they're using some weapon or device that stretches across the distance. Attacking someone on your flank raises your difficulty +2, while attacking someone behind you raises it by +3. Dodging characters may move up to 3" in a turn.

• Umbral or insubstantial characters are generally the only ones who can pass through a hex that someone else is standing in without confronting that second party in some way. Troupes might use a separate board for characters in the Umbra, or place slips of paper under the figures' bases to indicate that they're "not there" as far as other characters can tell. Spirits, as a rule, can fly up to 20 yards + Willpower per turn.

Alternate Combat Rules

Let him who desires peace, prepare for war.
— Vegetius

Combat rules have traditionally been complicated affairs involving pages of charts, modifiers, maneuvers and weapon damage tables. When your character's existence hinges on a few die rolls, such rules seem like a necessary evil. When a short battle intrudes upon a story, however, an abbreviated series of rules may be not only appropriate but, for troupe sanity, necessary.

This simple combat system, suggested by Christopher Kubasik in his excellent "Interactive Toolkit" series of articles (*White Wolf Inphobia*, issues # 50-54), takes the magickal feat and surprise maneuver rules one step further. Here, the player merely announces what she wishes to accomplish. The Storyteller decides the difficulty (and possibly the number of successes needed), and the player rolls. The success or failure of the event is based on that one roll. No charts, no modifiers. This system is quick and dirty, but dramatic. It's also wide open to abuse and extremely deadly. If you choose to use it, proceed with care.

Resolution

The simple combat rules work best when player characters need to work their way through a small army of soldiers, cyborgs, slaves, creatures, etc., to get to their main objective. Rather than rolling a long series of initiatives, attack rolls, damage rolls and soaks, the Storyteller and players decide to pass their fictional counterparts into the hands of Lady Luck. When combat begins, the characters get their normal initiative rolls. Each turn, both players and Storyteller decide what action their characters will try. Each makes their roll based on an estimated target number.

• If the character rolls three successes or more, he accomplishes that task

• If he rolls less than three, he was only partially successful.

• If he fails, he accomplishes nothing.

• If he botches, he hurts himself.

Combat objectives can range from stunts — "I want to knock him off his feet until he can listen to reason" — to minor injuries — "I'll shoot the gun out of his hand" — to mortal attacks — "I shoot him right in the face and kill him." The difficulty of the roll depends on the severity of the effect. The more difficult (or damaging) the action is, the higher the difficulty will be — and the higher the possibility of total failure. Success is not cumulative; the task must be decided each turn.

A complete success means the character did whatever he set out to do that turn. If he wanted to kill the cyborg, he did it. If he wanted to jump out and grab a chandelier, he does it. No problem.

A partial success means he did some damage, but not enough to finish the job. He shoots the cyborg; it bleeds a bit, but remains standing. He snatches the chandelier by his fingertips, but barely hangs on; he'll have to make another roll next turn or fall.

Failure is self-explanatory.

Willpower can be spent to gain one automatic success, but a victory cannot be gained only through Willpower points. The player must still roll at least one success. The automatic success rule does not apply. This system applies *only* to normal combat, not magickal fighting, although the Storyteller *may*, if she wishes, reduce the difficulty by -1 or 2 if some coincidental Effect is used (naturally, this still opens the doors for a botch and Paradox…).

Options

• If a player character is fighting cannon fodder, the Storyteller may decide to lower his difficulty or reduce the successes needed. If a major character (player or otherwise) is on the receiving end, she may offer that character a soak roll.

• If the feat involves more than one character (either dealing damage or taking it), The Storyteller may increase or decrease the difficulty or combine the Dice Pools and difficulties if she wants to. A pair of mages trying to kill three cyborgs at once may combine their Dice Pools and attempt to gain nine successes, total. The latter option may complicate things too much; if so, ignore it.

• The suggestion chart is based on normal humans. Large, tough or supernatural opponents may require more

Simple Combat Resolution Suggestions

Stunts

Objective	Roll	Difficulty
• Kicking in a door	Strength + Athletics	5
• Swinging from a chandelier	Dexterity + Athletics	5
• Yanking a rug out	Strength + Athletics	6
• Grabbing someone (or something) in motion	Dexterity + Athletics	6
• Scaring the crap out of someone	Manipulation + Intimidation	7
• Knocking someone off her feet	Dexterity + Athletics	7

Damage

Objective	Roll	Difficulty
• Disarmed	Dexterity + (attack)	7
• Hurt (equivalent to 1-2 Health Levels)	(appropriate Traits)	7
• Wounded (3-4 Health Levels)	(appropriate Traits)	8
• Instant knockout	(appropriate Traits)	8
• Death (or severe wound)	(appropriate Traits)	9

successes to harm, while smaller targets would require less. Really potent weapons (chain guns, grenades) might lower the attacker's difficulty by -1 or 2, while really weak weapons (switchblades, zip guns, rocks) would raise it.

Again, this system is designed for speed and simplicity. If it causes delays, complications or arguments, refer back to the usual method.

Making an Interesting Character

Statistics are abstract portraits; the collections of dots and Trait ratings reflect a larger picture of a person with specific talents and abilities. Who *is* that person, though? What can we do to turn that list of dots into a shaper of reality? What makes a **Mage** character cool, fun and memorable?

There are two types of characters in most fiction: *Stock* and *Personalities*. Stock characters aren't usually very interesting and do little more than perform a role in the story (person on the street, clerk at the store, librarian), acting within some basic demeanor (friendly, hostile, stupid, clever, arrogant and so on). The details of these characters are completely irrelevant to the story at hand, since such minor roles are only good for providing flavor to the important characters' setting. A good example of this kind of character would be Toht, the Nazi villain in *Raiders of the Lost Ark*. He's an interesting sideline, but without Indy there to give him his just desserts, he's nothing. He has no personality of his own, he's simply a type. Many Storyteller characters will be Stock types.

Players' characters, on the other hand, should be Personalities — strong, unique characters. Any interesting character, whether very simple or very complex, must have at least one of three things: Charm, Depth or Identifiability. If she's got two or more of these things, so much the better. Three, and she's a sure winner

• Charm

Charm is probably the hardest quality to fake. If you can pull it off, however, it's the aspect of your character that people will remember most. Going back to *Raiders of the Lost Ark*, take a look at Indiana Jones. He's got little depth — he's "Everypulphero," rugged, handsome, smart. He's doesn't have much identifiability — how many of us are whip-handling, lost-treasure-seeking, Nazi-trashing Ph.D.s? What he does have, in spades, is charm. He's got a sense of humor, wit, sophistication and a good heart buried under a tough shell. In short, Indiana Jones is someone that everybody would like to know.

The easiest way to make a character charming is, of course, to be charming yourself and just let it rub through (the way Harrison Ford's natural charm rubs through Indiana Jones). The secret for the rest of us, however, is to steal from real life. Almost everybody has met someone who was charming — think back to what it was about that person that was so attractive, then give your character that quality. Then, when playing the character, think to yourself, "What would this person do in this situation? How would he or she react?"

• Depth

Depth refers to a certain amount of intriguing complexity. Real people usually have somewhat muddled personalities with conflicting desires and goals. Good fictional characters can have all these things too. Depth implies a certain amount of trivial detail — knowing where and when your character was born, what her on-the-job life is like, how she relates to her neighbors, what kind of car she has, and so on. The more trivia you work out, the easier it will be to form her picture in your head.

If she dropped out of high school after falling in with a rough crowd, for example, she probably felt alienated or dissatisfied with her peers and went looking for others. If, in her search, she Awakened, what effects would this have on her? Was she happy to find the society of mages where she "fit in," or is she just as alienated from them? Most of the time, reams of in-depth information aren't interesting in and of themselves. They are, however, helpful when determining what your character is like and what she'll do in a given situation.

Don't, by the way, mistake unhappiness for depth. A character who's miserable all the time is just as dull and flat as one who's always happy. Her *reaction* to pain or unhappiness (or happiness and prosperity) is what gives her depth.

As strange as it may sound, depth is not always as necessary as it seems. A flat character with a lot of charm or identifiability (Indiana Jones, James Bond) can sustain interest for quite some time. However, depth *is* necessary for a character to survive and endure.

• Identifiability

Most people want to see themselves reflected in a character — either the way they are or the way they'd like to be. One of the reasons Indiana Jones is such a popular character is because many people would like to be like him: strong, smart, confident, superbly capable and attractive, but not superhuman. He's a Renaissance Man without being untouchable. Most people feel they have strong points in one or two areas — they're quite athletic or very smart, for example; the traits they don't have (but wish they did), they look for in fictional characters.

Similarly, most people are interested in characters who have traits they can identify with. This can be tough, though, because there are all kinds of people, and they don't always want to hear about other types. Intellectuals are generally interested in hearing about other intellectuals, but other people quickly get bored. Most people, however, do feel like life is a struggle, so they want to hear about how others have met — and conquered — adversity.

Our characters are extensions of ourselves, whether we want them to be or not. To a degree, this is unavoidable; roleplaying characters are like Rorschach tests — they show more about us than we realize. The best such extensions, however, take our self-image and go into orbit with it. So, when creating your character, a good way to make him interesting is to give him some aspects of yourself — ideas, attitudes, physical characteristics, interests and so on. Be sure to give him some qualities that you don't have, but would like to, however. If you're scrawny, make him tough; if you have trouble getting along with people, make him gregarious and friendly, and so on.

Rotes

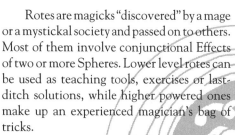

Rotes are magicks "discovered" by a mage or a mystickal society and passed on to others. Most of them involve conjunctional Effects of two or more Spheres. Lower level rotes can be used as teaching tools, exercises or last-ditch solutions, while higher powered ones make up an experienced magician's bag of tricks.

The following rotes are common ones among Council mages, and have been grouped by Tradition and power level. Game system notes can be found in the brackets at the bottom of each listing. Most groups use variations of these basic forms under different names, often performed with different styles and foci. As mages advance in enlightenment, most see rotes as needless crutches. Nevertheless, most Masters keep a few such "spells" in mind; after all, why not benefit from someone else's work? You never can tell when a rote might come in handy….

Akashic Brotherhood

Ricochet (• Correspondence, • Forces, • Matter, • Time)

Earnest students of Do develop exquisite awareness of missile weapons, both those they throw and those hurtling at them. A broadly trained Disciple of Do can redirect an arrow in flight or bounce a balanced club off of several surfaces before it strikes the target. Unarmed Akashic Brothers with a gift for improvisation use this skill to throw handy small objects into opponents' eyes.

[With a successful Dexterity + Athletics or Dexterity + Do roll (difficulty 5), an Akashic Brother can throw or kick any object so that it hits a target after multiple rebounds. Each success gives one bounce. He must know all of the Spheres involved to perform this feat. If he does, however, no magick roll is required. This takes a full turn.

[Against incoming missiles slower than a bullet, the mage's successes are subtracted from the attacker's successes before determining a hit. If the Brother rolls more successes than his attacker, the missile may be sent back the way it came! The Effect does not work on bullets or energy beams, and unbalanced objects may require from one to three additional successes. This rote often gives a damage bonus due to surprise.]

Mindfulness of Wrong Thought (•• Mind, • Life)

Some Chantries of the Akashic Brotherhood consider sensitivity to danger a marker on the Way to Ascension. Masters encourage it in pupils by striking them from surprise with wooden swords during chores, meditation, chants or sleep.

An Adept of the Order of Hermes, Francesca Inez Garcia y Hernandez, once entered such a Chantry for covert study of the Brotherhood's secrets. She carried her disguise well until her master leaped at her with a sword, and she reflexively called down a lightning bolt. In the aftermath, some in the Chantry argued for her expulsion, but the master revived in time to defend his disciple. Ultimately, Garcia y Hernandez left on her own when she found that the Brotherhood had no secrets she could comprehend.

[The rote alerts the meditating mind to hostile beings in the vicinity. The magick roll is made after the mage succeeds in a Perception + Meditation roll. One success on the magick roll indicates general danger and rough direction. More successes identify the threat's nature and location.

[The Effect reveals only immediate danger (that is, imminent in the current scene) to the meditating mage, and only threats coming from a living being with hostile intent. A similar Effect, substituting Matter 1 for Life 1, identifies traps, deadfalls and other inanimate perils.]

Pass Calmly (•• Mind, •• Correspondence, • Life)

With this Effect, the admirable Master Joro passed freely among agitated crowds, sensing and calming each person's turmoil. "Imbalance in the body fosters unsureness," he often said, "but the mind guides the body." With this rote, one of Joro's disciples, Ikana the Ronin, tried to make an enemy drowsy during battle. Ikana found that although the mind guides the body, his foe's mind was unfortunately intent on guiding his body to kill Ikana.

[The rote calms all Sleepers in a radius of two yards per success rolled. It does not work in combat.]

Celestial Chorus

Spy's Stigmata (•• Life, •• Prime, • Correspondence)

Paranoid mages have long known ways to detect magickal surveillance, but in 1934 Sunday Lynn gave the idea an original twist. Lynn, who Awakened during a snake-handling rite in rural Tennessee, suffered harassment by anonymous local Technocrats. When she detected them eavesdropping on her with Correspondence Effects, she cast a rash on them, marking their foreheads with a cross. Mages of other Traditions adapt this technique to create rashes in different shapes: sigils, the mage's initials or (in the case of one Virtual Adept) the Mark of Zorro.

[The mage needs only two successes to cast the rash, but the target may use countermagick to cancel successes one for one. The rash (actually a bacterial infection) is harmless, but can only be healed with Life 2 magick. This Effect is usually coincidental, and lasts for the normal duration (see the **Damage and Duration** table).]

Quietsong (•• or ••• Mind, • Entropy)

In the 16th Century, Letitia the Venerated took a rare opportunity to study with an Adept of the Euthanatos in Calcutta. Sadly, her mentor was not as chaste in mind as she, and he conceived a great passion for her. After developing this spell of mental stewardship, she broke with him; in retaliation, her master, Hasan Naraswami, tried to attack her. In his failed attempt, Naraswami suffered a Paradox backlash and succumbed to Quiet. Letitia sang her Quietsong hymn, entered his mindscape and guided him back to reality.

So say those of the Chorus. The Euthanatos claim Letitia suffered Quiet herself when first trying this spell. Naraswami used it to guide *her* out.

[At Mind 2, the mage perceives the Quiet victim's interior experience and altered reality. At Mind 3, the rescuer may enter a catatonic victim's trance (see "Quiet; Mindscapes," pg. 179). A successful Wits + Enigma roll (difficulty 7) lets her communicate normally with the victim. That victim, however, interprets the mage in the context of the Quiet illusions. He may, for example, regard the mage as a hobgoblin or internal demon.

[The mage cannot bring the victim out of Quiet instantly, and does not necessarily learn how to do so. She may, however, gain some understanding that helps her guide him out.]

Consuming Thought (••• Mind, •• Prime)

Benedetto Chiarezza used this rote to powerful effect during the medieval Italian conflict between the Guelph and Ghibelline factions. Benedetto, a Guelph, told selected opponents that their sins would lead to horrible tortures in the afterlife. The unfortunate Ghibellines found they could think of nothing else for days at a time. Driven to desperation, the tormented Ghibellines often deserted to Benedetto's faction.

[The rote forces a target to think a particular thought to the exclusion of all others, save for thoughts related to the target's immediate survival. The number of successes on the Effect roll determines how long the thought obsesses the target (the spell's duration). The target may resist the Effect with willpower.]

GROSTI·LOK95

Cult of Ecstasy

Psychometry (•• Time, • Matter)

Every object holds traces of its history and the emotions experienced in its presence. When a Cultist of Ecstasy touches an object, she can sense the object's background and notable events that occurred in its presence. Beginning Ecstatics can sense only during altered states of consciousness, when they may find it difficult or pointless to distinguish truth from imagination.

[The number of successes on the Effect roll determines how far back the assensing reaches (see the **Time Sphere** chart). Information gained is usually hazy and fragmentary: glimpses of a former owner, snatches of emotional conversation spoken in the object's presence or quarrels where the object got thrown. Most groups, including the Technocracy, have variations of this rote.]

Joyride (•• Correspondence, •• Entropy)

10 years ago, Cultist "Bourbon" Jan Treelinck got involved in a high-speed car chase through Amsterdam; accounts differ as to whether Jan was chasing Men in Black or being chased by them. Jan improvised a coincidental Effect that controlled traffic lights on his route. Later codifying it as a rote, Jan and his cabal took to wild rides at top speed through heavy traffic.

[All parties in a chase who know this rote roll Arete (difficulty 5). The mage with the greatest number of successes controls local traffic lights for one turn. With Mind 2, a willworker can also reduce traffic, within limits — although a loud and fast joyride often produces this effect without magick!]

The Moment That Stretches (• or •••• Mind, ••• Time)

Indonesians speak of *djam karet*, "the hour that stretches" — the flexible time schedule of clerks, porters, bureaucrats and others who keep citizens waiting. The Cult of Ecstasy, influential in Southeast Asian rites such as Malaysia's annual Thaipusam ritual, borrowed this phrase to describe a rote that dilates the Cultist's subjective sense of time. At the height of an ecstatic trance, a mage can think an hour's or day's thoughts in a few moments. The body remains at the slower time scale, rendering the mage immobile.

A trivial inversion lets the mage re-experience the sensations of a whole meal or extended debauch in one tremendous instant.

[At Mind 1 the mage affects only his own time sense; at Mind 4, the mage can affect someone else's. For each success past the first, the individual's subjective experience of a one turn interval moves one line down the **Duration** chart, to a maximum of one story. For example, three successes means the individual experiences a day's worth of thought in one turn.

[Cult philosophy dictates that the target of this Effect must always be willing, although the rote itself does not require this. The New World Order uses a malign variant as an instrument of torture.]

Dreamspeakers

Spirit Roster (•• Correspondence, • or •• Spirit)

The Dreamspeaker drums quietly, listening to the silence between beats. In her trance she hears the names of spirits active in the vicinity; she feels their auras. She breathes deeply, and with the indrawn breath comes the knowledge of their whereabouts. The drum beat: the rhythm of Gaia's thoughts.

[The rote identifies and locates any nearby spirit-beings (fomori, Garou, materialized spirits and so on). Spirit 2 lets the willworker communicate with them. The number of successes rolled determines the maximum practical range before sensory overload masks Umbrood activity. Under most circumstances, each success allows her to scan one yard. If she has some close familiarity with a particular spirit-being, or with the area she is scanning, her range becomes that of the **Correspondence Range** table.]

Gremlins (•• Entropy, •• Spirit)

This rote offers one symptom of the Dreamspeakers' changing nature, which many other Traditions call madness. During World War II, legends of "gremlins" (mischievous spirits that interfere with machinery) arose spontaneously among Sleepers, despite the Technocracy's best efforts. Dreamspeakers in urban areas exploit these legends to summon actual gremlins, visible only to Awakened beings. The Sons of Ether find gremlins intensely distasteful; some even call them "cruel to machinery." Virtual Adepts destroy gremlins on sight, as they would a cockroach.

[Summoning a gremlin requires at least three successes on the Effect roll. Each additional success doubles the number of gremlins summoned. A gremlin is a Storyteller character with Attributes of 2, Technology 3, Computer 1, Willpower 4 and three Health Levels. It has the Charms **Materialize**, **Control Electrical Systems**, **Short Out** (makes machinery inoperable) and **Ruin Software** (causes software programs to develop bugs). Unless it Materializes, the spirit cannot be seen by mortal sight. Most demand some kind of bribe before they go to work. Gremlins often remain for the magick's duration, and aren't choosy about whose machinery they wreck!]

Walking Chair (••• Matter, ••• Spirit, •• Prime)

Developed by the Dreamspeaker Four Arrow Cougar shortly before — some say shortly after — he entered a lasting Quiet, this highly vulgar rote animates furniture, appliances, toys, puppets and other lifeless objects. Each evening, as Cougar started drumming, all the tables and chairs in his home began to dance. "It looked like a cartoon," said his disciple, Alex Twelvetrees, "until the Antlered Men (Paradox spirits) showed up." The spirits carried Cougar away, never to return, but Twelvetrees' judicious use of the rote in battle has had some success.

[The number of successes on the Effect roll determines both how many objects may be animated (one for every two successes) and how long they remain so. Generally, this works for one turn per success, but never lasts more than a minute.]

Euthanatos

Safecracker (•• Entropy, • Matter)

Using this routine rote, a mage opens a safe by randomly twisting the combination lock's dial. Mages socializing in a Chantry or the Digital Web sometimes play a parlor game, listing all the different ways they can break into a safe: blowing it open, rendering it insubstantial, rusting it, comprehending that at the Correspondence Point it is no barrier and so on.

[For each success rolled, the mage learns one digit of the safe's combination. The mage needs one additional success to defeat a time-lock mechanism.]

Return to Darkness (•• Entropy, •• or ••• Forces)

Euthanatos Disciples admire this rote for its coincidental elegance. By causing failure in many components, the Effect extinguishes all light and power sources in an area when the mage shoots out or breaks a single lit light bulb.

While fighting Men in Black in the New Delhi airport, Srivasi Parananda used this sudden darkness to decisive effect. His cabal was ready with night-vision Effects or Correspondence sensing, giving them a decisive element of surprise when the entire terminal went black. This presented no danger to Sleepers; as usual, all New Delhi flights were on the ground and hours behind schedule.

[The blackout lasts for the spell's duration. The more successes the mage rolls, the wider the area that he plunges into darkness — two successes covers a room, four a building, eight a small city. Large areas require greater mastery of Forces magick.]

Chronopathy (•• or •••• Time, ••• Mind)

This anonymous rote of telepathy across time is quite old, but went into eclipse in the Renaissance. The Euthanatos Adept Constanza Perugia used it to experience the dying moments of countless predecessors. This, she thought, would lead her to Ascension. However, multiple death experiences caused a drastic Quiet. Constanza died at the hands of many hobgoblins, and their mischief led to witch-hunts and mass hysteria throughout northern Italy.

[By adding **Telepathy** to **Past** or **Future Sight**, a mystick can try to experience things that occurred in the past. The more remote or removed the time or person, the more successes the magick requires. Sleepers' feelings are easiest to detect; doing the same with an Awakened being's thoughts demands an extra success or two (or more in the case of an arch-mage or elder vampire).

[By using Time 4 to isolate a thought in time, the mage may send a message, image or emotion into the future. The message either arrives at a certain time, or is triggered by some specified event. ("The first three people to walk through this door will hear my warning.") Anyone who enters the mage's current location will telepathically receive the message at that time. The mage cannot know in advance whether a sending is received. The number of successes determines how far ahead in time the mage may send the message, or how precise its trigger will be.

[The Effect cannot capture experiences that were themselves gathered via chronopathy (so-called "second-order" experience). Only actual "first-order" experiences are accessible.]

Order of Hermes

Experience Substance (•• Mind, • Matter)

Attribution of this medieval rote remains in dispute. Moderates in the Order of Hermes suggest that all of the many claimants developed it independently. The matter has waited in the Pending file of the Attribution Committee's Dispute Adjudication Subcommittee for six centuries.

By rubbing a medicine, drug or chemical between her fingers, a Hermetic mage mentally experiences its effect. Hallucinogens inspire visions, while narcotics produce sleepiness and reduce pain, and so on. Medicines such as purgatives and diuretics produce only mental sensations, not the physical effects themselves. The mage remains in control, and can always stop the experience without harm, addiction or physical effects.

Cultists of Ecstasy sneer at this rote, for it produces only a pale simulation of the substance's reality. Its control is the antithesis of Cult doctrine. A Manhattan Cultist named Just Larry has modified this rote to amplify a substance's effects when actually ingested. He will presumably report results when he emerges from his coma in Bellevue Hospital.

[For dangerous substances such as acids, the Effect works when the mage touches the substance's container.]

Heat Trace (•• Time, • Forces)

The Order of Hermes scrupulously credits the creators of most rotes, documents their uses and annotates their variants. Phoebe Tetramegestus of Chantry Sangreal (Marseilles) developed this simple Effect in 1443. With it,

a magus tracks a living target based on the trail of slightly warm air his body leaves. The Forces Sphere lets her track the target beyond the immediate area permitted by the Time Sphere's retrocognition.

For this Effect, Phoebe received a Prix d'Honneur in the next Decennial Adjudication ceremony. However, she seems never to have used it, nor any of her many other inventive rotes. In the last nine decades of her life, she never left her Chantry.

[The number of successes on the Effect roll determines how far the mage can track the target's movements. Two successes covers the immediate vicinity, five successes a block, 10 a small town and 20 a city. The spell must be used within five minutes of the target's passing, or the trail fades — unless, of course, no other living thing or weather pattern has passed through the same area.]

Banish Elemental (•• Forces, •• Spirit)

For all their command of natural forces, Hermetic mages have a skittish relationship with elemental spirits. Dreamspeakers and some Verbena maintain respectful (if not relaxed) friendships with these volatile beings, but the Order's attitude toward many spirits ranges between hostility and contempt.

Cardinal Nunzio Blanco, a delegate to the Vatican under Pope Gregory XIII, devised this rote in 1576. Controversy erupted in later centuries when the Order debated adding Nunzio to its White Roster of Celebrants. Some mages argued that Nunzio had created this spell at the behest of the Order of Reason, forerunner of the Technocracy. Intense maneuvering led to Nunzio's addition and to the "accidental" destruction of all evidence that would settle the question.

[This is a vulgar Effect; each success rolled inflicts a Health Level of aggravated damage on an elemental spirit (if it's Materialized), or subtracts two points of its Power (if it's in the Umbra). This rote does not work at all on other kinds of Umbrood.]

Phosphoric Marker (••• Forces, ••• Life, • Correspondence)

Helga Zalau of the Romany created this vulgar Effect in 1339 under the name "Greek Life-Fire." The rote causes every living being in the vicinity to glow brightly but intermittently, like a firefly. The mage can omit herself and her companions from this Effect, making it useful during firefights.

[The number of successes determines how precisely the mage can control the glow. With only one success, ambient bacteria, dust mites and insects set up a general concealing glow. With three successes the mage can restrict the Effect to humans, and with four she can pinpoint all desired targets.]

Sons of Ether

Instant Measurement (• Correspondence, • Matter, • Mind)

Most new Son of Ether students quickly learn to read the hand-held Etheroscopic Property Analyzer. The ability to automatically measure an object's exact composition, weight and density proves extremely handy around the laboratory. In a trained user's hands, the Analyzer can also detect hollow hiding places or things hidden in containers that make them unusually heavy.

[The Storyteller may require a Perception roll (difficulty 4) to detect these hollows. The Analyzer is not a Talisman but a focus that makes the Effect coincidental.]

Pass for Normal (•• Mind, •• Prime)

After a ten-minute session under his Neuropathic Stabilizer, Scientist Stanford Latch could chat pleasantly at cocktail parties, stand in grocery lines and even talk to unmarried women without once launching into an exposition of the workings of his Neuropathic Stabilizer. Other Etherites joke about Latch's social inadequacies, but the issue of *Paradigma* that describes his device has quietly become one of the most popular back issues.

[This Effect adds one dot apiece to Wits, Expression and Etiquette. The Prime ensures that the subject's thought processes remain modified even without conscious attention. The successes determines the Effect's duration (see chart).]

Point-to-Point Narrow-Band Transmission (•• or ••• Forces, •• Correspondence)

The Technocracy has widely adopted this rote and has introduced the concept to Sleeper society; however, the Sons of Ether developed it in Britain during World War I. While wearing a delicate headset, the user can broadcast to any single nearby radio or television receiver, so long as it is turned on. This also works on close groups of receivers, such as those in a store window display. Whereas the Sons pre-empt existing signals, the Technocracy has used the rote to subtly alter existing programs, "customizing" them to deliver warnings, suggestions, false impressions and such.

[The number of successes rolled determines clarity of reception. The mage can make the voice or image sound and look like whatever he wants. The more elaborate the alteration, the more successes it demands. Correspondence 2 extends the range out of the caster's immediate area. With Forces 3 and Prime 2, the willworker can broadcast to receivers that are shut off or broken, although this Effect is vulgar.]

Verbena

Deduction (• Life, • Mind)

By sensing the small details of a stranger's life pattern and integrating them using sharp insight, a Verbena mage can decide whether the stranger represents a threat to her ░░░░░░░░. ░░░░░░░░░░░░░░░░░░░░░░░░░░░ rote a pop-culture spin by expressing their conclusions in the manner of Sherlock Holmes: "I perceive that you are left-handed, dabble in watercolors, were once a member of the Merchant Marines, and have recently visited India." Showing off with this rote around the coven is considered bad form.

[For each success rolled, the difficulty of an accompanying Mental, Intuition or Enigmas roll is reduced by -1. See "Abilities and Magick," Pg. 174 for details.]

Jack in the Green (••• Spirit, •• Life)

Mysticks must often travel to dense forests to contact the Glade Children (tree spirits) who dwell there. However, a diligent Verbena mage can communicate with a Glade Child in a park or city street, although the Umbrood spirit is usually torpid and decrepit. The mage sacrifices a few drops of his blood at the roots of a tree, then chants quietly. A bubbling cauldron produces best results, but pungent vapors of any kind may rouse the spirit, traditionally known among the Verbena as "Jack in the Green."

Jack is usually a good information source, but his gossip varies with the season. Jack notices many nearby events in spring and summer, fewer in autumn; in winter he's too sleepy. His memory, however, is long and excellent.

[The plant spirit often has Willpower 7, Rage 3, Gnosis 8, Power 20 and the Charms **Cleanse the Blight** and **Forest Sense**. The number of successes determines how long it takes to rouse the spirit and how cooperative it is. Communicating with a rural oak in summer requires only one success; rousing a city sapling in the dead of winter may require seven or more successes. Roleplaying influences this, as can successful Charisma + Etiquette rolls. An added bonus, like a burst of vitality or a sudden bloom (Prime or Life 2), might convince the spirit to be more cooperative.]

Thorn Wall (••• Time, •• Life, •• Prime)

Verbena prize this traditional Effect but restrict its use to "friendly" Horizon Realms to avoid Paradox. Using a thorn branch as a wand, the witch clasps it tightly. Blood from her hand drips over the wand and onto the ground. Where it falls, dense thorn bushes spring up, their branches waving and whispering. The witch, who controls the shape and area of the bushes, usually forms them into a barrier wall.

[Those who enter the barrier take three normal Health Levels of damage, but will not lose levels below Crippled. Depending on how the target reacts, he may end up stuck, ripping himself up further when he tries to break free. By channeling in Prime 3, this damage might become aggravated instead.

[The number of successes rolled determines how quickly the wall appears: one success, an hour; two successes, 10 minutes; three successes, one minute; four, 10 seconds; five

or more, instantly. It lasts for the normal length of time, then dies and crumbles.]

Virtual Adepts

Eavesdropper (•• Correspondence, •• Forces)

The Virtual Adepts have always been masters of the telephone system. Using this Effect, an Adept simply picks up a touch-tone telephone, punches in a mere 15 or 20 digits, and hears what's said within 10 feet or so of any other single working telephone of her choice, anywhere in the world. The targeted telephone need not be in use at the time, nor need the Adept know its location, just its number. (An Adept of Correspondence can project her senses to a known location without using Forces.)

In the Technocracy, the Syndicate and (especially) the New World Order execute this Effect coincidentally through expensive foci. Virtual Adepts simply exchange bootleg telephone access codes with feverish haste. A single code works for all desired locations, but the codes change once or twice daily.

[The number of successes indicates the audibility and clarity of the remote conversation. One success reaches telephones in the next room, five anywhere in a city, eight nationwide, and 10 worldwide. The Adept must know a current access code. The Storyteller may simply assume the Adept knows the code, roleplay its acquisition or roll Intelligence + Computer (difficulty 8) to determine if the Adept knows.]

Mental Interface (•• Correspondence, •• Forces, •• Mind)

Early rumors of this recent rote, designed by the famous Adept Dante, indicated that it dispensed with the computer altogether and let the user interface directly with the Digital Web. After those inflated expectations, the reality proved disappointing, though few mentioned this where Dante could hear it.

The program, with accompanying hardware modifications, actually lets an Adept's computer remotely sense and analyze the tasks another computer is executing. The mage can read documents being edited in a word processor, discover secret cash outlays in a Syndicate spreadsheet or learn a rival Adept's programming secrets. (Note, however, that many mages use equipment shielded from such surveillance with countermagick or Correspondence Effects.)

Dante's docco for the Effect discusses resonance theory and advanced telemetry techniques, but as Disaster Master puts it, "Blah blah blah, look, just tell me how to run the program, okay?"

[The rote is coincidental. Once the link is established, it lasts for the rote's duration. The storyteller may require Wits + Technology, Computer or Science rolls to analyze the results.]

**Boot Buzzer (•• Correspondence, •• Forces, or •••
Forces, •• Correspondence, •• Prime)**

A mischievous or vindictive Adept on a network is a frightening figure. He can alter a computer anywhere on that network to deliver a powerful shock to its user. The Adept usually prefaces the jolt by putting a strange image or sarcastic message on the user's screen.

After the Effect is cast, it takes several minutes to accumulate the electricity needed for the jolt. With Forces 3/ Prime 2, the charge can be created instantly. With Time 4, the Adept can delay the jolt to a certain time, such as when the user turns the computer on or types a particular word.

[The Adept must, of course, locate the target successfully through Correspondence magick; only then can he set the charge. For each success beyond the first, the jolt inflicts one normal Health Level of damage on the victim, although the Forces 3/ Prime 2 variant inflicts the usual Forces damage.]

Public Posting (•• or ••• Mind, •• Correspondence, •• Prime)

Typing furiously (high adrenaline appears to improve the rote's power), the Virtual Adept broadcasts a simple message (usually "Help!") or some straightforward emotional sentiment ("Screw the world!") in such a way that all mages within range can hear it, with or without a computer of their own.

[The number of successes determines the range and clarity of the sending. One success reaches adjacent rooms, three a city block, five a small town and eight a city. With Mind 2, the message becomes an empathic sentiment; at Mind 3, the message can be detailed and specific.]

Mages of Note

Pleased to meet you,
Hope you guessed my name.
— Rolling Stones, "Sympathy for the Devil"

The following mysticks are well-known throughout Awakened society, mages whom even their enemies respect. Though by no means the most powerful mages alive (or the only ones of note), each has a reputation which precedes him or her. Player characters may cross paths with these notables, hear about their adventures or even choose one as a mentor or connection at the Storyteller's option (five points worth, of course). Such "celebrities" will not, of course, be at a player's beck and call, but may offer some last-minute aid — or opposition.

Tradition Masters

These are only the tip of a very large iceberg; each Tradition naturally has its favored celebrities. These Masters, however, are familiar to most young Council mages in the Western world, if only by reputation.

Master Porthos, Drua'shi Master and Deacon Primus of Chantry Doissetep

Amid the twisted intrigues of Doissetep, Master Porthos stands like a battered icon — spat upon, ancient, worn, but compelling. One of the oldest Tradition mages alive, Porthos strives to leave a legacy to atone for the Ascension he has never attained.

A Hermetic mage almost from childhood, Porthos actually Awakened on his own and joined a Hermetic House decades before the Grand Convocation. He has seen the endless parade of triumphs and frustrations the Council has endured and is responsible for a number of both. His conscience often troubles him, but he remains a solid figure in Council politics, doing whatever need to be done to further the Traditions' ends. A relentlessly moral man, he considers himself unworthy of the power he has accumulated and drifts in and out of sanity.

Porthos' power is almost unimaginable. On his infrequent visits from the Shard Realm of Forces, he radiates an aura of otherworldly might even Sleepers can detect. The hobgoblins his frequent Quiets manifest keep Doissetep... interesting... to visit. Through force of personality, magickal prowess and longevity, Porthos holds onto the leadership of the Drua'shi, the *de facto* rulers of Doissetep. Though rival cabals besiege these "Seekers of Truth," no conspiracy has dislodged them for long. Despite these triumphs, this Master claims to long for death. His recent book, *The Fragile Path: Testaments of the First Cabal*, is supposedly his farewell to this incarnation. If he has a death wish, however, no would-be assassin could attest to it. Porthos still clings to life with the ferocity of a mad god.

Czar Vargo

Indisputably the leading scientist of the Sons of Ether, Czar Vargo was born Vargo Zamtredia on the Black Sea coast, in what is now the Republic of Georgia, in 1878. Apprenticed to Count Roland of France, Vargo displayed astonishing talent with Forces and soon mastered Matter as well. He developed his conversion engine by age 19 and a preliminary version of his gravity ray soon thereafter.

At the Paris Exhibition in 1900, Vargo spoke publicly against the world's preparations for war. Soon thereafter, he disappeared. He emerged dramatically on July 24, 1914, when fleets of his airships appeared over seven major cities and demanded that all national governments surrender their arsenals to him. His superior science overcame all Sleeper opposition, and only the Technocracy's desperate assault with steam-driven robots and mutant soldiers drove him away.

Vargo's ships retreated into the sky, presumably past the Horizon. The New World Order removed all evidence of the takeover attempt from the historical record, while Paradox backlashes destroyed entire budding technologies. Since then, many observers (including Void Engineers) have reported sightings of Vargo's fleet in the Deep Umbra. Czar Vargo's current whereabouts and occupation are unknown.

Najjda Bantu

An African Celestial mage, Najjda resigned from the Council during the days of the Triangle Trade. A century later, she helped found the Underground Railroad in the U.S., fought the forces of the Confederacy, then returned to her homeland to "encourage" the English and German settlers to leave. After the Ahl-i-Batin left the Council, Najjda's allies convinced her to return to Horizon. She has been a fixture on the Primii Council ever since.

Despite her Tradition's affiliation with the Judeo-Christian religions, Najjda has always identified the One as a goddess whom she calls Bau-Hatt. Over 300 years old, she retains her vigor and transforms into animals to watch over her chosen people. Though never wholly pacifistic, Bantu has avoided excessive violence throughout her centuries of struggle. The turmoils in central Africa, however, have wounded her spirit. She has brought rain and purged sicknesses on more than one occasion, but realizes that her battle cannot be won alone. From the Council, Najjda seeks a united effort to end Africa's suffering. So far, her companions seem bent more on warfare than welfare, and she grows more discouraged with each year.

Within the last five years, a contingent of Dreamspeakers and Choristers has answered Najjda's call. Their recent quest to eradicate the Progenitor laboratories in Zaire has won attention and acclaim from younger members of the Council.

Dante

Virtual Adept Desmond Collingsworth, AKA Dante, was born on 07/21/1969 in Chicago. Collingsworth is said to have Awakened before birth. Guided by the Progenitors, he graduated high school at eight, Harvard at 13 and medical school at 18. Before the Technocracy could recruit him, however, he was kidnapped by a band of Adepts called the Lab Rats, each a former Progenitor breeding project like himself. Learning the ways of magick from them, Dante soon independent and began recruiting children that Progenitors had earmarked as recruits. Most of them he gives

over to Tradition allies. Others he sets up in hidden safe homes with mundane identities.

Dante carries himself with the cool assurance that comes of supreme competence in a limited domain. In the Digital Web, Dante has become somewhat of a legend. His Mastery of Correspondence, Forces and Mind has not prevented him from socializing with "lesser" mysticks. For Dante, any person has infinite potential. He has dedicated himself to helping as many folks realize it as he can.

Alexis Hastings

A tinkerer and a traveler, Alexis has won a strong reputation among her chauvinistic Etherite colleagues through meticulous research, ingenuity and pure nerve. Though personally shy and apparently conservative, Hastings' enthusiasm for Science knows no bounds. Notorious for her love of electricity, Alexis publishes frequently in *Paradigma* and scopes into the Net for R&R (rest and research). At present, she's hard at work on an Otherworlds overview, detailing her findings and experiences about travel beyond the barriers.

Kibo

Much like Demonseed Elite and the similar "Captain Feedback," Kibo is a semi-mythical idol of the Virtual Adepts. Kibo definitely lives, physically, but no one knows his true identity or location. Kibo's fame lies entirely in the Digital Web. There, he uses impressive Correspondence magick to appear or cause strange events wherever his name is invoked. These tricks are mischievous rather than malicious and sometimes beneficial.

The Adepts have taken to calling Kibo "the god of cyberspace" and have founded a silly but elaborate religion, Kibology. Those outside the Tradition find Kibology baffling, unsure whether it is a joke masquerading as a religion or a religion masquerading as a joke. The Order of Hermes currently states that Kibology is a religion masquerading as a joke masquerading as a religion.

Marianna

Archmage Marianna oversees Balador, the supreme Cult of Ecstasy Chantry, and its surrounding Horizon Realm city of Altua. A Master of Correspondence, Life, Matter, Mind and Time, Marianna hardly looks her age (believed to be 76). Instead, she reshapes herself week by week, taking on the appearance of ideal beauty in a succession of current and historical cultures: Berber, Javanese, Hollywood, Khmer, Hopi, 1920s Paris, 1600s Elizabethan and a thousand more. Her duties as supervisor of the Tellurian's greatest pleasure house evidently have not exhausted her. Marianna's continual zest for sensation is remarkable.

In recent years, Marianna and the Balador cabals have declared a vendetta against a diabolic cult known as the

Seventh Generation, which (she claims) has deliberately corrupted sexual practices in the eastern United States. The Order is unclear as to what kind of sexuality Marianna could think corrupt, but she has, among Council mysticks, proven herself a worthy and sensible ally and an archmage of astonishing power.

Raging Eagle

A mysterious martial artist Master of the Akashic Brotherhood's order called the Scales of the Dragon, Raging Eagle has apparently lived many lives, going back to the Himalayan Wars between the Brotherhood and the Euthanatos. In his current incarnation, Raging Eagle trained in Colorado, mastering the most destructive aspects of the Do. He believes he is fated to die whenever he fights for more than a week. Though Raging Eagle is undoubtedly conscientious and means well, he is prone to deep Quiets and furious changes in temperament.

Sam Haine

The true name of this Verbena mage is unknown; "Sam Haine" is, of course, a punning reference to the ancient Samhain festival. The Verbena also call him "Changing Man" because of his variable appearance. He is said to travel the world searching for mythic elements of reality and taking them to Verbena Horizon Realms for preservation. He also delights in debunking false occult items and ideas that the Syndicate promulgates among Sleepers.

Iconoclastic to an extreme, Sam Haine consciously flouts the typical Verbena rituals and trappings. Verbena mages claim he has allies or sympathizers within the Technocracy, because he has been captured several times and escaped each time. An enigmatic figure to Tradition mysticks, Sam Haine seems to enjoy the confusion he inevitably leaves in his wake.

Heasha Morninglade

Though young by archmage standards, the Verbena Heasha has won a significant reputation through her eloquent dedication to Ascension's ideals. In an age where few aspire to any purpose higher than the accumulation of power, Morninglade's arguments and writings have inspired Sleeper and Awakened alike to follow some higher goal.

The last apprentice of Nightshade, Heasha benefited from that Primus' centuries of wisdom and folly. She learned, as few others have, of the Council's founding struggles and has an uncanny insight into history. Nightshade, whose vision helped shape the Traditions, may have passed on more than her Arts and learning; some older mages claim that Nightshade can still be heard in Heasha's impassioned rhetoric. Whatever the truth may be, Morninglade is a formidable willworker for her age. Though not quite 40, she commands the Spheres with the skill of a magus centuries older.

Heasha holds no formal Council rank, nor does she want one. Politics bore her. Nor has she chosen a formal apprentice. Instead, she often travels with a pack of mysticks in a mobile Chantry called the Magic Bus, offering a helping hand — and stern wisdom — to mages in over their heads.

Tom "Laughing Eagle" Smithson

A former Apache shaman, Tom Smithson leads the Lodge of the Gray Squirrel, a four-cabal Chantry of Native American origins located in a Horizon Realm called the Second World of the Diné. Smithson's origins are obscure, but it is common knowledge that he was enslaved for decades in the horrendous Technocracy Construct Null-B. Escaping with four other Dreamspeakers, Smithson returned to Earth and joined the Circle of the Gray Squirrel in 1958, the first non-Navajo shaman to enter the cabal.

Through great ability, honorable conduct and generosity, Smithson rose to Mastery of Spirit and Adept rank in several other Spheres, and to leadership of the cabal called the Cult of the Bear. He is plain-spoken and outwardly cynical, but has repeatedly shown compassion and friendship to mages of other Traditions.

Smithson and the Bear Cult work both on Earth and in the Otherworlds to protect Native American people and beliefs, and are said to have many werecreature allies. Smithson himself investigates Horizon Realms of Technomancers, tutors young mages and raises horses. He has argued for a united assault by all Traditions on Null-B, but to no avail.

Technocrats

The Council keeps its most detailed files updated with Technocratic Masters. Unfortunately, this information is often subverted by the Union's scrambling and disinformation magicks, false reports and the almost supernatural awe with which low-ranking Technomancers regard their superiors. The mages below are only a handful of these dedicated foes of dynamism.

The Matriarch

The union of two Iteration X sisters, the Matriarch commands the dreaded Construct of MECHA, a forced labor camp/prison from which the Technocracy draws much of its Classified Bio-Harvested Quintessential Force (Tass). This mage is said to exist only within MECHA's massive internal systems, though she supposedly attends conferences in Autochthonia and travels into the Web for brief, savage forays.

The Matriarch is a technocratic nightmare, an omnipresent Big Sister who monitors her Construct with

unblinking eyes and punishes failure with methods that cause even cyborgs to tremble. Hated and feared within the Technocracy itself, the Matriarch nevertheless epitomizes Iteration X's ideal of perfection — eternal unity with The Machine.

Andre Takahashi

The Syndicate head of the Far East, Takahashi has perfected the art of personae. With advanced bio-alteration (Life magicks), he switches identifies and nationalities to whatever suits him. Under aliases, Takahashi is thought to govern three yakuza families, the Wo Group Triad, a Nepalese liberation group and a Brahmin clan with a lineage going back over 2,000 years. Whether or not André killed off the original leaders or simply used Mind influence to "convince" others that he belonged is a mystery.

Records trace Takahashi to a marriage between a French tradesman and a female samurai in the late 1800s. He learned secrets from a number of mystickal societies before joining the Matsuba-kai ikka shortly before W.W.II. There, he encountered a Syndicate cell and devoted himself to the Union's cause. When the Technocracy switched sides during the war, he personally undermined the Japanese defense, then fostered U.S. economic interests before turning their best methods against them. Although he concerns himself largely with "legitimate" corporations, Takahashi has found the underground elements to be a superior form of damage control.

André is a formidable man, versed in sorcery, technomagick, economic control and street violence. Few who meet him realize it at the time; Tradition cabals have clashed with crime families in Asia, Europe and the U.S., only to find some lead back to one of Takahasi's many personas. Only infiltration, data raids and a bit of André's egotism have allowed the Council to recognize him at all.

Oscar Hamilton

After the death of Null-B's chief commander Alonzo Vendiz, Hamilton quickly rose to the top of a bitterly divided Triumvirate. The Construct, which has weathered persistent Marauder attacks, has become famous throughout the Union for its battle-readiness and combat savvy. Hamilton, a high-ranking NWO operative, is the main reason for Null-B's survival.

A graduate of the NWO's top-ranked training academy, Hamiliton served as a Man in Black from World War II until Watergate, when his identity was compromised by top-secret tapes. He moved to the then-powerful Construct to serve as Vendiz' second in command and led the powerful shock-troops to victory after victory before a massive Marauder assault rocked Null-B in 1993. Since then, the outlying war Construct has suffered badly at the hands of flying Umbral horrors and internal dissent. Rumor has it

that Hamilton assassinated Vendiz himself, but the mess the killing has left makes this unlikely.

Hamilton carries great weight with the Inner Circle. A brilliant strategist, he has coordinated raids against Horizon itself, and once forced the Council headquarters to move several of its Nodes to avoid being cut off. A quiet man with an unassuming demeanor, Hamilton hides his war-savvy well. Those who know him, however, speak of an inhuman vitality and deep commitment to reality deviate extermination.

Dr. Ken Himiitsu

This unorthodox Technocrat fills an important post: the preservation of the Union's interests in San Francisco. His unusual theories and occasional compromises have earned him enemies and grudging respect from both Council mages and the Doctor's colleagues.

Himiitsu is a visionary; he is not above striking alliances with mysticks or investigating wild new theories if that helps him protect his Sleeper charges better. He will not tolerate any threat to the people under his protection, and can be harsh if necessary. In general, however, he prefers to work things out peacefully, and will offer compromises that seem treasonous to more dedicated Technocrats. To him, the common good is an ideal worth any sacrifice.

A massive man, Himiitsu directs the U.C. Medical Center with a firm hand. His physical strength, affable manner and powerful friends earn the Doctor a respect out of proportion with his actual abilities. Like many Progenitors, he keeps a variety of clones around for risky situations. Unlike most Technocracy leaders, however, Himiitsu is not afraid to get his hands dirty if need be. He will place himself — or his clones — in danger if personal involvement is called for.

Eva Raum

An energetic and visionary woman, Raum spearheads the Void Engineers' earthbound operations. With her friendly disposition and charisma, she garners support for her passion — the exploration and classification of known space. An amazing capacity for organization, mastery of Correspondence, Mind and spirit-tech, and complete devotion to the Technocratic cause make Raum a driving force on both sides of the Gauntlet.

Eva knows what's out there; during stints with both the PDC and the BDC, she encountered horrors beyond any filmmaker's nightmares. The revulsion she feels for these defilers inspires her to pursue the Pogrom whenever such "aliens" appear. Outer space, she feels, is the hope of the future, an endless palace of wonders and resources. To make space safe, however, the aliens must be taught a lesson: The Earth will not tolerate invasion. Compromise invites chaos.

Those who meet Ms. Raum would never guess at her fanaticism. A master of P.R., she attends private and governmental functions, raising funds and enthusiasm for the conquest of space. Though in her mid-50s, Eva has energy and looks that put supermodels to shame. Within the Conventions, she carries healthy respect for her quick thinking and boundless knowledge. A joke among the Engineers states that Raum never sleeps, she simply lets her clones do it for her. There may more truth than fiction to the claim.

Weaver

A semi-mythical entity which dwells in the Umbral reflection of San Francisco, Weaver is said to have been a Orphan shaped by the Technocracy into a guardian of the Bay Area. Through its control, the geological instabilities of the city have been stabilized. No one wants to think what may happen if Weaver were disturbed or destroyed.

Hackers into Technocracy databases have found many references to Weaver, but few hard facts. Most sources refer to Dr. Himiitsu with veiled comments and innuendo, a discretion unusual to the literal-minded Technocrats. No one seems to understand Weaver's exact function or nature. All data, however, suggests that the entity is something best left undisturbed, for the city's sake.

Terrance Whyte

Few outside the NWO's Colleguim of History can claim to have met this elusive historian. Though his writings indicate an Awakened mind, he is known more for his dissertations and lectures than for his magickal skill. Whyte's uncanny knack for documentation, however, indicates that he possesses — or at least *seems* to possess — great skill with Time influence.

Whyte's writings are famous throughout both the Union and the Council. He holds a steadfast devotion to the Technocratic cause and insists that, given the chaos reality deviants provoke, the Pogrom was the only logical solution. Among the many accounts of the Ascension War, Whyte's are held to be the most reliable — if biased — documents available.

Wild Cards

These shadowy mages play many sides of the field. Though they seem to hold alliances with certain groups, each pursues his or her agenda over all others. These mysticks may appear as allies one story and enemies in the next. Handle with care.

Secret Agent John Courage

This rogue Man in Black seems to have preferred a life of adventure to the boredom of a Technocratic routine. The epitome of the super-agent, Courage refutes the common wisdom that all Men in Black are soulless drones. He's changed sides more times than anyone can count. It's only

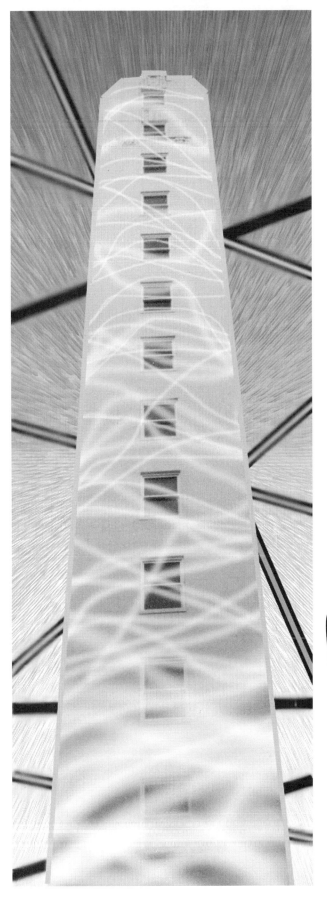

because of his almost preternatural senses, fantastic luck and impenetrable Arcane powers that John Courage is alive at all. Though he tops the Technocracy's hit list, many among their rank-and-file admire Courage and let him "miraculously" escape capture.

If John Courage is confused by his own skewed agenda, he doesn't let it show. Though his actions are flamboyant in the extreme, his demeanor is always calm and secure. No obvious feature separates Courage from any other Man in Black. He has not, as of yet, met his demise, so his skills must exceed his compatriots' by a very wide margin. No one knows why Secret Agent John Courage does what he does, but wherever trouble beckons, he cannot be far behind....

Jodi Blake

An infamous Nephandus, Blake rarely appears the same way twice. Her favorite forms seem to include beautiful children, seductive young women, male rock musicians and strippers. Though supposedly a Tradition *barabbi,* no one knows exactly where or when she came from.

Subterfuge is Jodi's game, and she plays it well. Even the Dark Ones do not trust her; it has been said that over 40 mages have fallen through this tempter's manipulations. Whatever form she takes, Jodi prefers physical beauty over combat prowess and subtlety over violence. Centuries of life have taught her dozens of skills in addition to her magicks, and she can outmaneuver most younger opponents through sheer wit. When forced to fight, she often takes the form of some animal, attacks and flees.

Demonseed Elite

The Virtual Adepts use the handle "Demonseed Elite" to refer to an early Master who supposedly worked for Bell Labs in the 1970s. By means unknown, this Master merged with the global telecommunications network, living entirely in its cable and satellite links. Since that time, he has physically manifested as "a giant orange monster truck" that runs down his enemies.

According to the Adepts, Demonseed is omniscient and extremely hostile to on-line vandals, whom he considers "lame." The Adepts recount tales of disemboweled or lobotomized hackers. These resemble urban legends, and the Council itself has not yet verified the existence of Demonseed Elite.

Robert Davenport

Dr. Robert Davenport is the most famous Marauder in existence. While the Tellurian echoes with rumors of Mad Ones in Shangri-La, rocs on space stations and Chaos Oracles in Greece, the only name *everyone* seems to know is Davenport's, and the only confirmed fact anyone can get hold of is that he is the leader of a strange, powerful and ever-changing group of crazies known collectively as the Butcher Street Regulars.

Those who claim to have met him say he is an older man (hair color varies by the eyewitness reports), slightly taller than average and very charismatic. Lucid, reasonable and apparently favorably inclined towards the Traditions when in his saner states, he is a master of tactics, a remarkable leader (i.e., he can keep 12 or more Marauders together and focused — more or less — long enough to be effective) and distressingly likable. Less-experienced mages are advised, should they encounter the group, to retreat to a safe distance and let the Regulars do their stuff. Mere Adepts probably can't stop them, and it's no good sticking around just to die in the Paradox backlash.

The Regulars themselves, met singly, are less dangerous — perhaps. Two of the group are supposedly lying open on dissecting tables in the Progenitors' labs, taken down by three mundanes with automatic pistols. On the other hand, Mama Goose, a well-known and powerful zooterrorist, is said to run with them, and the Islington Horror (a manifestation of unknown but considerable power) has been reported at the scenes of four BSR attacks.

The Technocracy, of course, wants Davenport dead. Attacks believed to be orchestrated by him eat away at a small but annoying portion of their operations every year, and the situation is embarrassing. The Syndicate has offered a substantial bounty for his verifiable death (both in mundane terms and to the attractive tune of 1,000 Tass), but so far no claimants have come forth.

Jennifer Rollins

Though trained by Verbena and Ecstatic Mentors, this wild card chose neither group. Instead, she wanders the Earth looking for insights and novelty. Originally an artist, Rollins extends her talents to her magick, weaving Prime, Life and Spirit affinities into a primal Orphan style.

Rollins is an intuitive mystick rather than a scholarly one. Her training has been short and eclectic — some say that a Nephandus took her as his apprentice before she killed him. Though barely 25, she commands power out of proportion with her short Awakened life. Those familiar with Avatars say Jennifer's is quite strong; she is clearly destined for great things. Many groups have tried to get their hands on her, but she has little to do with any of them. She follows her own Path.

Sarcastic and direct, Rollins is eccentric, even among Orphans. Fond of body art, she sports a variety of tattoos and piercings. A collection of faded scars on her arms betray her most common focus — rune blood magick. She wanders barefooted in ragged neo-hippie clothing and is said to have friends among the shapeshifters, though no one has actually seen her with any. Ferally attractive, Rollins still has a somber side even the Cult could not lighten. Though she makes friends easily, she never settles for long. Jennifer Rollins is the quintessential Orphan — primal, tragic and loaded with potential.

Chapter Two: Shadows in the Rain

Woke up in my clothes again this morning
I don't know exactly where I am
And I should heed my doctor's warning
He does the best with me he can
He says I suffer from delusion
But I'm so confident I'm sane
It can't be optical illusion
So how can you explain
Shadows in the Rain?
— Sting, "Shadows in the Rain"

Introduction

"Shadows in the Rain" is an introductory setting for **Mage**. Both background material and story ideas are included. Although most of the information pertains to the city of Seattle, the description centers around a Chantry hidden under Pike's Place Market, an area located between downtown Seattle and Elliot Bay. While the Technocracy has thoroughly influenced the city (especially through their ties to a local aircraft manufacturing company), there are other groups in Seattle that are just as dangerous and hostile to Tradition mysticks.

Themes and Motifs

The Sleepers who live near downtown Seattle are unaware of the dangers that surround them. Occultists study horrific magicks, monstrous creatures stalk the night, and behind the scenes, a secret society known as the Technocracy weaves its subtle web of control over both the enlightened and the mundane. In the midst of this madness, a hidden group of mages watchfully guard against the coming of night. The Cubbyhole Chantry isn't large, but their altruism and vigilance has kept their neighborhood alive.

The mages described here are all students or custos who reside in the "Theater of the Mind" (see pp. 35-42) while serving and protecting their Chantry. Visiting mages will have a chance to see the benefits and drawbacks of a large Chantry. The Theater is filled with politics and rivalry, complications and diversions, but it also has a wide variety of resources for characters who want to become part of the Seattle scene.

The setting is well-suited to multi-faceted adventures. While Seattle is a considerable city, it isn't huge, and outside the city limits, suburbs quickly disappear and give way to wilderness. The downtown area is perfect for stories that require a gritty urban setting, while the wild is an ideal atmosphere for surreal and mysterious encounters. (Snoqualmie, the real-life setting where *Twin Peaks* was filmed, is only a few hours away.) There are also possibilities for politics and intrigue. Although the conflicts in the Chantry are slowly getting more intense, most of the members are still very motivated and quite loyal to the Chantry's founder, Rudolfo Ouspensky.

The dominant motif here is the juxtaposition of dynamism against stasis. The unusual is often found in the midst of the commonplace. Strangeness breeds in Seattle. Pike's Place Market swarms with mundanes — tourists, shoppers and merchants conduct their business with great vigor — but it also attracts more than its fair share of eccentric and bizarre people. On the weekends, the crowds of Sleepers try to leave the banality in their lives behind them, and the neighborhood comes alive. On the surface, the community buzzes with a mixture of conformity and energy.

Behind the scenes, few Sleepers realize the *real* energies at work here. Hidden in the teeming masses, supernatural forces watch, wait and sometimes act. The mages of the Theater of the Mind want to keep the chaos and energy alive in the neighborhood, but they have to keep it under control, too. Their task is complicated by the internal bickering that occurs whenever large groups of people work or live together. Even so, these mages feel a degree of responsibility to their community. A large part of that is motivated by a survival instinct. By keeping their neighborhood safe, they keep themselves safe. Two dominant themes, then, are community and survival.

The local mysticks are at a distinct disadvantage in protecting themselves: the area is a target for Marauders who want to unleash their madness on an unsuspecting populace, but it's also surrounded by enough witnesses that Technocracy agents have an edge in conducting investigations. If the mages here can't keep the neighborhood safe, the Technocracy will resort to more extreme methods to police the area. Tourists have cameras, merchants become territorial, and locals can become inquisitive. For Tradition mages in this area, discretion is the better part of survival.

The Neighborhood

While downtown Seattle isn't that different from the downtown of any other gritty urban metropolis, the area around Pike's Place Market is a little cleaner, a little nicer

and a lot more oriented toward shoppers and tourists who want to mingle in a friendly, happening environment. A few blocks away, affability gives way to the slightly morose and stand-offish attitudes affected by many of the locals downtown. On a sunny day, spirits rise… but most of the year, sunny days aren't terribly common.

The amount of rain that allegedly falls in Seattle has been exaggerated… slightly. Not every day is rainy, although the weather often has a cold, murky, Gothic feel for weeks at a time. Rain is common enough and light enough to be ignored by the Washingtonians who live there. It's not unusual for someone not to notice it's raining until several minutes after he's left his front doorstep. Light jackets and trenchcoats aren't terribly common, but only a tourist would carry an umbrella.

One reason the rain and cold is endurable is the constant availability of all forms of coffee. Mocha, latte, Americano and even (gasp!) drip coffee (preferably blended) — you name it, it's here. In Seattle, even McDonald's sells espresso.

East

Two blocks east of the market, Second Avenue has the feel of any other street downtown. Buses pass by every few minutes, the homeless ask for change, and businessmen sip their espresso. Mundanes rarely nod at each other when they pass on the street; freaks welcome their brethren. For most of the year, people resign themselves to the lack of sunlight, the slight cold and the occasional rainfall. Many residents, in fact, prefer things that way.

On First Avenue, the austerity of downtown gives way to a colorful row of shops and businesses. The diversity is quite evident, ranging from the Hotel St. Regis and Nordstrom's department store north of the Market to the Lady Lust Theater south of it. The more notable locations include the office of a psychic reader, a store specializing in New Age and environmental merchandise, several trendy clothing stores and a few bookstores and gift shops.

Although Seattle has the feel of a small town, the "homeless problem" in Seattle is comparable to what one would normally find in a much larger city. There are a few missions between Pike's Place and nearby Pioneer Square, one of which is tended by Morgan Celeste. The charity reduces the suffering somewhat, but some visitors still aren't quite sure how to react to the constant requests for change. Most hurry past and hope to avoid conflict as much as possible.

West

The street that runs along the west side of the building, Western Avenue, runs steeply downhill. As it passes by the Market, it descends from a small park at the north end of the building to the bottom of a flight of stairs at the south end. A massive parking garage is available, and a few blocks away, traffic from the city's highway, I-5, rushes past on an elevated expressway.

Elliot Bay is two blocks west of the market. There are more shops here, but these are set inside huge buildings built atop piers jutting into the bay. Along Alaska Way, tourists and shoppers can stroll along a boardwalk stretching from one shopping plaza to another. Among the attractions are several large seafood establishments, the Seattle Aquarium, tours of nearby Puget Sound and countless opportunities to purchase momentos of one's visit.

Immediately to the suothwest of the market is Armory Park. On weekends, vendors surround the area, tourists relax on benches, the homeless sleep on the grass. Once in a while, a "mall preacher" or street musician will stand on a hill in the middle of the park to address the assembly. The Space Needle can be seen to the northeast.

South

Immediately to the south of the market lie the Harbor Steps: a stairway as wide as a city street leading from the open-air market to the bottom of Western Avenue. Across the street from the top of the steps is a local celebrity: the Hammerin' Man.

The Hammerin' Man is a four-story black metal sculpture that resembles a cut-out figure. He holds a long piece of metal in one hand and a large mallet in the other. Powered by a motor hidden in his back, he slowly hammers away, over and over and over. A wide stairway that leads to Second Avenue is a known gathering place for Marauders.

One block south of the statue is a two-story black-and-white mural of another local celebrity. The image of Jimi Hendrix looks out on the bay, surrounded by psychedelic shapes and figures. Cultists of Ecstasy have been known to stop and puff a few salutes in tribute.

Pike's Place Market

From a distance, the Market doesn't look terribly large. A huge neon sign on the corner of Pike Street and Pike Place advertises the "Public Market Center" in 10 foot high neon letters. Directly below the sign is the main entrance to the building.

- **Pike's Place**

This street runs along an arcade located on the top story of the Pike's Place Market. Traffic from cars is light; traffic from pedestrians, however, is heavy on the weekends. On the east side of the street, a series of shops sells everything from tie-dye T-shirts to Turkish delight. On the west side of the street is the market itself.

- **The Arcade**

The top floor of the Market is busiest on the weekends. Fish merchants scream to passing customers, and fresh seafood rests on beds of ice. Street musicians compete for the crowd's attention, vendors hawk from tables, farmers sell their produce, shoppers wander by in droves, and eccentric locals mingle in the crowd.

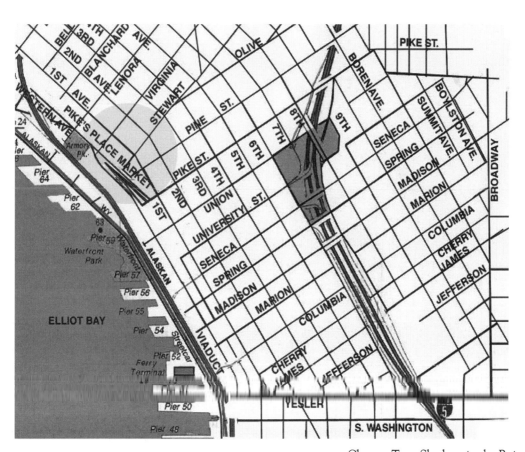

There are a few signs posted to encourage patrons to help "Save the Market." The establishment was almost destroyed in the early '70s until the community came to its aid. Since then, the merchants running the market have kept their home alive by using a number of unusual strategies. The most unusual can be found at the corner of Pike Place and Pike Street — parents and children often stop to put spare change into a four-foot-high brass piggy bank.

The Interior

The architecture inside the building dates back to 1907. A long walkway of ramps leads through six stories of shops and stores. Getting lost is extremely easy, but that does encourage tourists to stick around a little longer. Many of the merchants here specialize in the unusual. Browsers can examine Egyptian decorations, rare movie posters, antique dolls, collectible comic books, rare books, Native American artwork, French pastries, Japanese artwork, wind-up toys and other assorted curiosities.

• The First Floor

The first floor of the building adjoins Western Avenue. The shops down here don't get as much traffic as the stores along the Arcade. Most customers don't enter the building from the ground floor, so the stores here cater to customers looking for high-priced items, such as antiques or specialty items. The least frequented store, it would seem, is a magic shop sequestered in a corner of the first floor.

The Conjurer's Cubbyhole

Buried in the first floor of the marketplace, deep inside the labyrinthine structure, is a small and fairly modest shop called the "Conjurer's Cubbyhole." The entryway itself is fairly nondescript, and the sign above the door has worn away over the years.

No one would ever know the store was here if it wasn't for a rather garish theatrical poster by the front door. The top of the poster screams out in neon letters the name of the store's owner: "Rudolfo: The King of Magic!" A garishly painted scene proclaims Rudolfo's accomplishments as *The Acme of Mystical Prowess!* The owner has over 50 posters in his collection, and although the sign over the door hasn't been changed, the poster changes once a month. The latest display might show him levitating a scantily-clad woman over a pit of snakes, wrestling a giant gorilla, firing a pistol at a charging elephant, hanging in chains over a tank of water or one of the countless other spectacular feats he has (allegedly) performed.

The Cubbyhole has a wide selection of merchandise, both on the floor and in the "back room," but the store itself is exceedingly small. The wares here range from simple tricks a child of 12 could (almost) perform to professional supplies and a few collector's items. The selection of fake shrunken heads, Halloween masks, trick knives and bottles of stage blood adds a sinister touch to the atmosphere. In fact, the atmosphere gives most people the creeps. (It's reminiscent of the magic shop in *Pee Wee's Big Adventure*, although it's a little stranger, if that's possible.) Most people who wander into the store are judged by their reactions. Anyone who takes an Addam's-Familiesque delight in the store's strangeness is noted as being "one of the family."

Once in a while, some connoisseur of the macabre inquires about a particular collector's item. Those "in the know" speak of the Cubbyhole's unusually vast selection of curios. The occasional sale of one of these collector's pieces is really what keeps the store in business. The latest item on display is a Box of Knives, a sinister recreation of an iron maiden that resulted in the death of a magician's assistant 30 years ago. The curios often sell for unusually exorbitant prices, but periodically (and mysteriously), a piece is sold for a favor or another rare item.

Few people are invited into the "back room" where most of these items are kept. The door, marked "Private," is kept locked. There's a reason for the owner to be cautious — he's very particular about who he lets into the back. The greatest accomplishment of his career is the Chantry occulted behind his store.

The Conjurer's Cubbyhole is actually just a front for a Chantry run by Rudolfo. Although he's a Hermetic mage, his Chantry has members from most of the Traditions, and is a very popular meeting place for Hollow Ones. Rudolfo is a rather gregarious fellow. If the characters meet with Rudolfo's approval, the Storyteller should encourage the players to think of the Cubbyhole as a "second home." The troupe of practitioners that surround him are all part of his greatest performance.

Security

The shabby collection of rooms in the basement of Pike's Place Market doesn't attract many customers, but it's close enough to a high-profile shopping center to make it difficult for, say, an army of HIT Marks or Men in Black to march into the place without attracting Paradox or undue attention. Speaker phones connect the front counter to the back rooms, enabling people in the shop to communicate with people in the Chantry. The shop is fully owned by Rudolfo.

One side effect of the Chantry's magickal energy is a psychic disturbance that makes the establishment slightly more suspicious. Every once in a while, for no readily apparent reason, people attempting to go into the shop find themselves in another shop. Most of the time, they simply believe they made a wrong turn ("I meant to go into the Cubbyhole. Why did I come here? I guess my mind was wandering…."). However, visitors who make a Perception + Alertness roll, difficulty 8, have a clear memory of going into the Cubbyhole. Unless they have a reason to believe in space-time distortions, they'll get extremely confused. ("Wait… What's going on here?") Fortunately, it never happens to the same person twice in a row, and rarely occurs more than once every few weeks.

Behind Closed Doors

The walls of the back room are lined with a number of unusual devices. Up to 10 pieces sit on display at any given time. Among the most visible ones present now are: a square box that looks suspiciously like an iron maiden, a deep-sea diving suit, a large glass aquarium filled with murky fluids, a web wrought of black chains, a strait jacket suspended from the ceiling and a stuffed jackalope. Rudolfo will not reveal the story behind a display unless he believes the visitor is genuinely interested in acquiring it.

The back room of the magic shop adjoins the foyer of the Chantry. Its wall is entirely covered by a red velvet curtain. If visitors are lucky enough to be deemed worthy to visit the Theater, Rudolfo, with suitably dramatic flair, will part the curtains and reveal a rolling wooden door. This door is a Talisman that separates the mundane dimensions of the back room from the fantastic space-time distortion (represented by a swirling mass of vibrant colors) that leads into the Chantry's lobby. A visitor can only pass through if he possesses at least one level of Mind or Spirit, or if he's accompanied by a member of the theater troupe. A ceremony is required on stage before a mystick is acknowledged as a "member of the family." The door cannot be circumvented by the use of Correspondence. (The stats for the Talisman are Arete 4, Quintessence 20, Correspondence 4, Spirit 4, Prime 2.)

The Other Side

The area on the other side of the velvet curtain has a deceptive complication: the Realm is a bit larger than what the mages here require. The extradimensional building immediately behind the door is well-defined for less than a city block; beyond that, guarding the building becomes difficult. The exits lead to a series of tunnels that connect this Realm to others like it, but exploring these tunnels has proven to be somewhat difficult.

Shawn Cornell, the Chantry's resident expert in non-Euclidean mathematics and urban spelunking, can testify to the deceptive nature of the Umbral labyrinth. The sensors and traps he has set throughout the tunnels do little to forestall his nightmares of the horrors that may be contained below. The members of the Chantry aren't sure

which is more of a threat: the rival mages above, or the dangers that might lurk in the tunnels below.

At the center of this chaos, a group of mysticks try to preserve their safety and sanity. Intra-group stress and external threats have slowly turned them against each other, like rats in a shrinking cage. Tempers run high, and frustration boils. In the center of this performance is Rudolfo, the director of his troupe and the leader of a collection of eclectic and eccentric actors in his Theater of the Mind.

The Theater of the Mind

So you are interested in the unknown? We cannot keep this a secret any longer…

— The Great Criswell, *Plan Nine from Outer Space*

It's no wonder that Rudolfo was optimistic about this Realm. The ambiance and structure of this pocket reality was influenced by the artistic vision of the 1940s and reflects that era's grace and style. The main chamber of the Chantry resembles an opulent, old-style theater. Cream-colored walls, rococo designs, a hint of Art Deco and iron railings all add to the effect.

The Lobby

The theater lobby's rich elegance puts the utilitarian appearance of a modern movie theater lobby to shame. In that bygone age, no expense was spared to make a guest feel as though his visit was an important one.

On the ground floor, more glorious theatrical posters adorn the walls. Most of them advertise some of Rudolfo's most momentous performances and reveal a retrospective of his greatest (alleged) achievements. Beyond the red curtain lies a three-story atrium; elegant staircases lead escorted guests up to personal rooms on the two upper floors.

When guests arrive, one of the custos emerges from the cloak room and offers to check any outer clothing. A counter stretches between the two doors leading into the theater; another custos sits reading there most of the time. The brass eagle of a 30-year old espresso machine shines with pride behind him. Students who are too busy to find food elsewhere are quite grateful for the java and pastries available here.

If characters are invited to one of the famous Chantry meetings in the Theater of the Mind, they'll have a chance to meet at least five or six of the performers in the lobby beforehand. Such meetings are only called once a week, but what the gatherings lack in size, they make up for with intensity. Once a visitor enters the main chamber from this side, he'd best be prepared to argue well.

The Main Hall

Although the Art Deco decor is still intact, the theater has undergone a few renovations. Most of the seats in the hall have been removed, and only the first three rows are still here. The carpeting was replaced by parquet tiles from

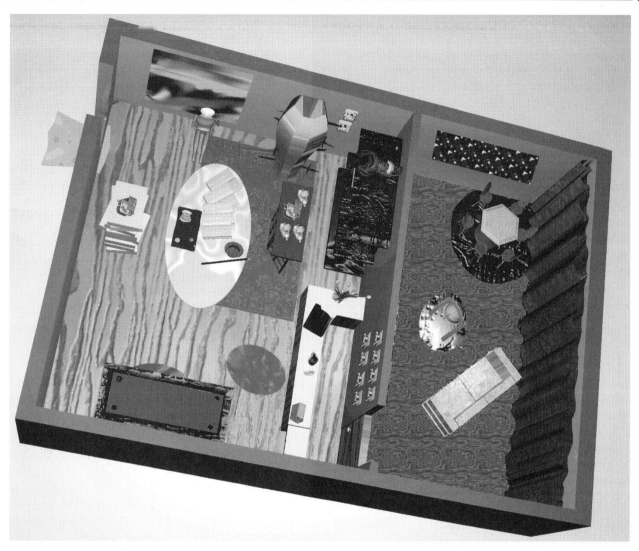

a visiting Arabian mystick in an effort to preserve the dimensions of the theater. (How long the enchantment will work is anyone's guess…)

By the back wall, a wooden loom displays the handiwork of Branwyn Elspeth, the leader of the Traditionalist Cabal. She adjusts the pattern in the threads from day to day. If one looks closely at her work, insights into the supernatural activity in the city are revealed. Unfortunately, Branwyn is usually frenetically busy; she'll bite the head off of anyone who looks over her shoulder as she works. She grows visibly agitated if spectators come anywhere near her; this lack of manners is her way of showing how terribly overworked and important she is. Despite this, she remains available to the members of her cabal, and she is extremely polite to possibly allies. Although she's a very vocal critic of Ruldolfo's policies, the Chantrymates she manipulates form the second strongest cabal in the city.

In the center of the chamber, a marble fountain harnesses magickal energies. The investment of effort and energy has paid off: the Chantry's Node has liquid Tass flowing through its glowing white water. This fountain actually combines four Nodes, and together they bring about 20 points of Quintessence into the Chantry each day. 10 points gather in the surrounding pool each day. (Psychics will notice the presence of the Tass if they can make a Perception + Alertness roll.) The rest of the energy is absorbed into the fountain's rock. From there, the energy sustains the structure of the Realm — not a drop spills onto the parquet tiles.

The first three rows of the theater have comfortable chairs, and performances are held on the stage at least once a week. If a visitor peers into the orchestra pit, the phosphorescent glow of computer screens reveals when Magnus, the Chantry's Virtual Adept, is present. The orchestra pit is more appropriate for him than a laboratory: he carefully programs the rows of synthesizers and recording equipment he stores down here. Magnus is famed both for his musical talent and his gift for summoning spirits. This has brought a great deal of criticism upon his cabal, especially from the more Traditional mages who frequent the establishment.

When his cabal's leader is patrolling the streets, Magnus usually acts as the spokesman for his comrades.

From the stage, you can easily survey all the activity in the main chamber. Not surprisingly, Chantry meetings are held here, and they're suitably dramatic. The energetic arguments of the two strongest cabals have never resulted in certámen duels, but they have, at times, come close. When the arguments start, the front door is locked. There's no point in locking all of the exits; anyone impulsive to storm out of the room would do so at his own risk....

The Tunnels

Rare indeed is the visitor who is bold enough to leave the theater from either side of the stage. Six exits lead from the theater, and all of them work. Two of them are deadly....

The two doors on the left side of the theater lead to the Chantry's library — an unassuming room overflowing with theater and movie posters, magazines and books both magickal and mundane. Mysteriously, the room changes its size each day, and the number of books present appear to change from week to week. As a side effect of the spatial distortion, the "interlibrary loan" results in the disappearance, reappearance and replacement of about 20% of the room's tomes each week. Very rarely, alternate or alien books will replace familiar ones. Shawn Cornell has thus volunteered to be the Chantry's librarian, as only his constant revision of algorithms can allow him to guess where reference materials are. (The difficulty of all Research rolls in this room increases by +3.)

The two doors on the right side lead into a series of hallways, which continue the architectural motif of the theater for several blocks. The space-time distortion on this side of the chamber seems somewhat contained as well, but the configuration shifts from week to week. The members of the Chantry treat it as they would an unpredictable hedge maze. Sometimes whispered discussions and intense arguments are carried on here, far from prying eyes. When Chantry meetings begin, the doors are locked. It's also rumored that two of the mysticks meet in the maze for more amorous reasons....

Leaving on either side of the stage can have tragic results. The exit signs flicker as the configuration of these tunnels change. Beyond the steel doors, stone tunnels seem to go on forever. Sections connect in strange and unusual ways, and interconnected locations baffle explorers unfamiliar with the Correspondence Sphere. Rudolfo is fairly certain that the Realm only extends as far as the city limits of Seattle. Mercifully, only one person has seen any type of creatures in the tunnels, but despite the efforts of Shawn Cornell, the tunnels *still* haven't been fully explored. Theoretically, *anything* could be down here.

Within the labyrinth behind the stage, two paths lead to the real world. Regardless of reconfigurations of the maze, Shawn can follow both of them quite easily. The first egress is a waterway that empties into the city sewers. Anyone trying to enter through the other side of the waterway experiences a disorienting psychic effect similar to the one customers feel in the Conjurer's Cubbyhole (described above). The second passage leading to the real world ends in a metal door leading to a transit tunnel. There are many such tunnels under downtown Seattle — several buses travel through them between eight in the morning and five in the afternoon. Shawn is pleased to know that there's a fairly dependable escape route from the Chantry. Secretly, it pleases him even more know that he's the only one who knows where it is.

Personalities

Got a gallery of figures standing in a row,
And every single figure has a soul of its own
— Oingo Boingo, "My Life"

The mages of the Theater of the Mind have polarized into two factions. Their agendas clash with little violence but plenty of emotion. Stage left is the Traditional Cabal, a group of introspective willworkers who want to build a "sensible" Chantry. Most of them prefer to wait and watch the situation in Seattle, focusing on problems involving mages and Sleepers nearby rather than complicating their lives with other supernatural problems. Stage right is the Renegade Cabal, a group of modern mages who believe that the Chantry should be more pro-active. They organize patrols, both above and below the Theater, to seek out problems and confront them. There's also the beginning of a *third* cabal: a group of disaffected practitioners who would just as soon forego both activities and focus on survival. The Hollow Ones in the neighborhood form the core of this third group.

Considering the youth of most of its members, the Cubbyhole has a good reserve of energy and magick at its disposal. With such resources behind them, player characters who deal with the Chantry have a chance to learn the levels of conspiracy and deception within the city. What they investigate, though, will affect how the three factions react to them. If they have no interest in the local vampires and werewolves, the Renegades will criticize them, but if they get involved, the Traditionalists will be concerned. A third resource also exists: the Outcast Clique at the Liquid Haze, a coffee shop downtown (see "Adventures"), which consists of three barely-Awakened (but street-savvy) Hollow Ones and four of their Sleeper friends.

Despite the clash, most people within the Chantry have developed a great affection for the place and the other people in it. One cabal in the Chantry (possibly the one that associates with the characters) creates trouble constantly. They aren't traitors *per se*, but more like problem children, constantly in trouble and continually bringing embarrassment to their "superiors."

The Shadow Box Players

Anyone visiting the Chantry has to personally cleared by Rudolfo. He has sought out practitioners with strong magickal abilities who are honestly willing to make the world a better place. Any new mysticks visiting the area have to prove themselves before he lets them into the "back room," but once he's decided he likes someone, he sticks by his hunches.

A group of performers — the Chantry's acolytes — work and sometimes even live here in rooms on the second floor. This troupe, the Shadow Box Players, has five core members and two additional "stagehands" who know the secrets behind this gig. These five artists — Sally Cornwall, Stefani Olsen, Larry Cook, Dawn Groseclose and Chris Russell — have years of dance, music, acting, gymnastics and stage combat experience. Rodolfo pays them well for their services, and Larry and Chris rarely leave the Realm at all. All five are sworn to secrecy about their gig, and would never compromise it. If the word got out about the theater, each one knows, the Players' fun would end for good.

The stagehands, CeeCee and I.J., come and go as they please (though CeeCee keeps rabbits in a room set aside for her use). Both work outside the Realm as well, and do freelance tech work for mundane theater groups. Like the Players, these Sleepers know that something extraordinary is going on in this fabulous place. They're easy-going people, but would give their lives to protect the Realm from the outside world.

Every week or so, the Players perform some new show for their hosts and any visitors. Some mages, especially Hype, Miriam, Magnus and even Rodolfo himself, get involved. These acts range from music concerts to three-act plays or magic (or magick) shows. Audiences are encouraged, though not coerced, to tip the players. In between shows and rehearsals, the Players keep the place tidy, practice, hang around or socialize with their mystick counterparts.

The Leaders

Rudolfo Ouspensky

The Chantry Leader

Nature: Architect
Demeanor: Caregiver
Essence: Pattern
Tradition: Order of Hermes
Attributes: Strength 2, Dexterity 2, Stamina 3, Charisma 5, Manipulation 4, Appearance 3, Perception 4, Intelligence 3, Wits 4

Abilities: Alertness 2, Awareness 4, Brawl 1, Computer 2, Cosmology 4, Culture 2, Dodge 3, Drive 1, Enigmas 4, Etiquette 3, Expression (stage magic) 4, Intuition (trustworthiness of others) 4, Investigation 3, Law 3, Leadership 4, Linguistics 3, Medicine 3, Meditation 4, Occult 5, Research 5, Streetwise 3, Subterfuge 3, Stealth 3, Science 1
Backgrounds: Allies 5, Arcane 4, Avatar 3, Chantry 3, Destiny 3, Dream 1, Library 3, Node 3
Spheres: Correspondence 4, Entropy 2, Forces 4, Life 3, Matter 3, Mind 4, Prime 3, Spirit 2, Time 1
Willpower: 8
Arete: 6
Quintessence: 9
Paradox: 2

Background: Rudolfo Ouspensky was born in 1937, and he's loved magic as long as he can remember. As a child in his native Czechoslovakia, he went to magic shows with his father. After the Second World War, his family moved to America. Entertainment was different there, but watching vaudevillian magicians sparked his imagination, and yearly visits from a traveling circus fanned the flames. As a freshman in college, he voraciously read every book on magic he could find. He never believed magic to be more than clever stage tricks until a fateful day in 1953.

On a cold December morning, Rudolfo sneaked into the workshop of a prominent stage magician to learn some trade secrets. His curiosity demanded answers. He had two choices in life: find the secrets he needed to make his dreams come alive, or expose magic as a sham and put it behind him. Hoping for the best, he caught the performer by surprise.

He found more than he bargained for: the magician opened up a suitcase, calmly stepped in and closed it behind him.

Rudolfo was stunned. He didn't want to disbelieve — in fact, he wanted to find out more. He picked up the suitcase, ran to his dorm room and set it on the floor. Then he waited. Eventually, as Rudolfo expected, the suitcase opened, and a very surprised magician stuck his head out.

"Where am I?" the mage demanded. "Who are you?"

"Your new student!" Rudolfo replied, and the rest, as they say was magic (or magick, as it were).

Five years later, "The Great Rudolfo" was ready to tour the world. He made a career of wowing his audiences with "Amazing Feats of Mystic Wonder!" With style and skill, he pursued the "Acme of Magical Accomplishment" as he traveled from one exotic location to another, fighting Nephandi, Marauders and Technomancers along the way. 15 years later, his youthful vigor and vitality finally began to ebb. He settled in Seattle, and began to create the Conjurer's Cubbyhole.

Since 1973, the Cubbyhole has been a haven for traveling Traditionalist mages who meet with Rudolfo's approval. The store is the same as when it opened, and Rudolfo hasn't changed much either. The Chantry, however, has grown and prospered. If only the Realm didn't keep growing, too....

Though he's a generous man, Rodolfo is no fool; his travels have shown him how dangerous the world can be, and he won't open the red curtain to just anyone. Once he's identified a mystick, Rudolfo has more respect if the prospective performer chooses clever illusions over powerful Effects. (After all, when you know magic, altering the universe would be cheating!) Most traveling mages will usually have to perform a service for the community before Rudolfo will take them into his confidence. He's very open about the fact that he prefers Hermetic magick to all other forms, but doesn't harbor ill will for any Tradition, save for the Euthanatos (whose "Good Death" seems to be nothing less than an excuse for murder). When he meets Orphans, he'll usually offer the talented ones a chance to join the Order of Hermes.

Although he's quite comfortable dealing with Chantry politics, the pressures of his fame within Council circles has influenced his approach to magick. With him, magick is a matter of "all or nothing." He can accomplish minor feats quite easily with simple stage magic, and he's busy enough to leave most essential tasks to his Chantrymates. When he pulls off an Effect, however, he always has to live up to his reputation. For that reason, he doesn't go all-out very often. When he does, he considers anything less than absolute perfection as failure. This leaves him slightly sad: he knows that if he fails, he must do even better next time. For that reason, he usually leaves the major castings to other younger mages, who "need the practice more."

Image: Rudolfo is a kindly man in his late 50s with a pleasant face and a ready smile. He treats just about everyone as a doting uncle would: finding out what they like and arranging to find it for them. He delights in the strange, and loves simple tricks. Since the store is fully his, he has the option of being as eccentric as he likes, right down to his choices in clothing.

Although his corpulent frame looks most at home when he sports a tux, tails and cloak, he usually prefers slacks, loafers and a sweater. Regardless of his accouterments, his stage presence is always evident. He leads by charisma, not guile. Rudolfo speaks with a slight Rumanian accent.

Roleplaying Notes: Gregarious and charismatic, you are the consummate performer. By putting people off-guard with your dramatic flair, you can take opportunities to test their reactions. You've got an intuition for human character, but any skepticism you hold hides behind an outgoing demeanor. Help those in need, but never give away your secrets easily. People must prove their good intentions before you'll risk the safety of your Chantry.

Every once in a while, you grow sad; the world was once a more romantic place. The lessons you have learned are more valuable than ever, now. Some might accuse you of hiding in your Cubbyhole, but you know that the hope and wonder you inspire will lead younger "students" — mage and mortal alike — to respect your Arts and the world around them.

Sanctum: Rudolfo has a small apartment in the Chantry containing everything he holds dear. He can afford the luxury of occasionally living in the past. His surroundings include photos, playbills, posters and newspaper clippings from his days on the stage, a personal library (that he won't risk in the Chantry's library) and other personal momentos. His current apprentice, a young woman named Lisa Yokahama, has an adjoining apartment, and runs the counter of the shop when Rudolfo's not there (she may be run as a player character). Lisa's increasing involvement with Hype, however, has him concerned.

Quote: *Mastery of the elements is easy. The Siberian rope-and-ladder trick — now that's difficult!*

Branwyn Elspeth
The Leader of the Traditional Cabal

Nature: Director

Demeanor: Child

Essence: Pattern

Tradition: Order of Hermes

Attributes: Strength 2, Dexterity 4, Stamina 2, Charisma 1, Manipulation 5, Appearance 4, Perception 3, Intelligence 3, Wits 3

Abilities: Alertness 3, Awareness 3, Cosmology 2, Culture 2, Etiquette 3, Expression 2, Intuition 3, Leadership 3, Occult 2, Subterfuge 4

Backgrounds: Avatar 4, Influence 3, Node 2, Talisman 4

Spheres: Correspondence 3, Mind 4, Time 3

Willpower: 8

Arete: 7

Quintessence: 5

Paradox: 1

Background: Branwyn has lived a life of isolation and meditation. Her father made sure she had everything she ever wanted… as long as she didn't want anything outside of her father's estate. As an introspective and neglected child, she invented elaborate fairy tales to entertain herself. She only had one other source of solace: her mother, who taught her to sew and weave.

As Branwyn sat alone in her room, both her fairy tales and handiwork became more elaborate. She told her teddy bears stories of a magical world that once was, but would never be again. As she stared into the warp and weave of the cloth she created, she could almost see it. And as her Avatar grew from senescence to sentience, she began to realize that her visions were not just fantasy….

Branwyn has an old soul — she is the reincarnation of an Order of Hermes magus from the 13th century. She has dreams of her previous life, and the only way to hold on to her sanity in the dark world of the 20th century is to try to recreate what once was. In this respect, her life really is a fairy tale, with herself as the central character. She's the lonely, beautiful maiden everyone should pity, the tragic heroine no one can rescue, and, first and foremost, a self-centered manipulative little rich girl who is determined to always have her way.

Image: Branwyn has the sort of beauty that can only be attained by endless vanity. Her looks are particularly plum for her age, which is somewhere in her early 20s. Her pale skin is a testimony to her isolation, not her innocence. Her azure eyes, like crystalline pools of sparkling water, belie the depths of her self-centered introspection, not her soulfullness. The luxurious blonde hair that cascades to her waist is certainly stunning, but it wouldn't be if she didn't spend at least two hours a day combing it. She prefers to wear clothes that she has sewn herself, for only she knows how to truly flatter her perfect figure. When she does purchase the inferior work of others, she chooses outfits with a medieval flavor.

Roleplaying Notes: Anyone who doesn't serve you is working for the competition. Play up your status within the Order of Hermes; after all, that's the easiest way to get Rudolfo on your side. Crusade against anything in the Chantry that is sexist or that gets in the way of what your female Chantrymates are doing; that's a quick way to get the other women on your side. Flatter the men around you, with a slight touch on the arm or a wan smile — you have the charms required to play off the insecurity of the boorish males around you. And, let us not forget, your command of the Mind Sphere doesn't hurt either.

Quote: *Why, how very clever of you! We're so lucky that you're here to help us….*

Hyperion, aka "Hype" (Francis Hyperion Keating)

Organizer of the Renegade Cabal

Nature: Judge
Demeanor: Loner
Essence: Dynamic
Tradition: Akashic Brother
Attributes: Strength 3, Dexterity 3, Stamina 4, Charisma 3, Manipulation 2, Appearance 2, Perception 2, Intelligence 3, Wits 4
Abilities: Alertness 3, Athletics (Skateboarding) 4, Brawl (Jeet Kun Do) 4, Do 2, Dodge 3, Investigation 3, Leadership 2, Medicine 2, Melee 3, Stealth 2
Backgrounds: Allies 3, Avatar 3
Spheres: Forces 2, Mind 2, Time 3
Willpower: 7
Arete: 4
Quintessence: 3

Paradox: 5

Background: At the age of 16, Hype starting running from his problems. A high school drop-out from a broken home, he took a job as a bicycle messenger in downtown San Francisco to support himself. For the next three years, his life was one big hustle. What began as a day job delivering documents became a dangerous night job as he started to deliver packages freelance. He was well aware that some of the deliveries he made were illegal, but the money was too good to pass up. As he surrounded himself more and more with the seedy side of the drug culture, Hype developed his own addictions: speed and danger, though not always in that order. When he wasn't on a bike, he was on a skateboard or running… whatever it took to take his mind off his own pain.

The more he took on and the faster he went, the worse his life became. He never thought; he just kept moving. Even with a fat bank account, Hype found himself mired in seedy criminal activities, deals gone bad and contacts burned.

It only took one person to turn his life around. One of the contacts he was making runs for was a Cultist of Ecstasy with a need for obscure herbs. "Fritz" was never in a hurry, and he had an uncanny way of getting Hype to stop long enough for a cup of tea or a five-minute break. Hype's potential was obvious, so Fritz set him up with an unusual mentor. The Akashic Brother who set him on his way was something of a visionary, and Hype's power and his talent at Jeet Kun Do reflect his teacher's skill.

Now, two years later, Hype has developed the powers of his body and mind. He still, however, has a taste for speed, an attraction to danger and a bit of an attitude. He also has a low tolerance for bullshit and deception, which means he'll gladly get in someone's face if he disagrees with them. The passive attitude of the Traditional mages in the Chantry is slowly grating on him, and he's beginning to take on more than he can handle again. Half the Chantry stands behind him in his efforts to "patrol the city," but his motivational skills don't make up for his lack of strategic thinking. In short, he's a half-assed leader. When something dangerous happens, he can get people to move, but getting them to move in the right direction isn't easy. He's great at uncovering problems, but terrible at solving them.

Image: Hype radiates energy, especially when he's standing still. Even in the most dangerous situations, he stays in control, but his confidence comes from his unlimited potential energy. He usually prefers to wear skanky shorts and neon short-sleeve shirts, even in the coldest weather, partly because it gives him an excuse to show off the many scars that he's taken from "bad asphalt." He loves to be shocking, right down to his green hair and bad tattoos.

Roleplaying Notes: Everything works on an emotional level. Once you're enthusiastic about something, nothing gets in your way. Stay in motion — the energy within you is too intense to allow you to sit still for long. Speak animatedly and persuasively. Commit — nothing is worth doing halfway.

Quote: *Yeah, well, while you were in here studying, I've found something. You want to hear about it, or should I just take care of it on my own?*

Chantrymates

Since Rudolfo is reluctant to get directly involved in many of the affairs of the Chantry, the other practitioners will take whatever leadership they can get. Most of them would be quite willing to help anyone new who seemed like they were willing to change things, but for the present, the best they can do is give information and advice.

Shawn Cornell
Master of Alternative Engineering

Faction: Renegade Cabal
Tradition: Son of Ether/ Nephandus-in-training
Nature: Survivor
Demeanor: Loner
Essence: Questing
Attributes: Strength 2, Dexterity 3, Stamina 3, Charisma 2, Manipulation 3, Appearance 2, Perception 3, Intelligence 4, Wits 2
Abilities: Alertness 2, Brawl 1, Dodge 2, Enigmas 2, Investigation 3, Linguistics (Arabic) 1, Melee 3, Occult 3, Research (Non-Euclidean) 4, Science 3, Stealth (Traps) 4, Survival 2, Technology (Sensors) 3
Backgrounds: Arcane 3, Avatar 3, Mentor 3, Node 2
Spheres: Correspondence 3, Entropy 2, Forces 2, Prime 2
Willpower: 6
Arete: 3
Quintessence: 2
Paradox: 5

Background: As an undergraduate in electrical engineering, Shawn was a very undisciplined student. His real talent lay outside the classroom. Using whatever scraps of electrical equipment he could scrounge, he was a master of low-tech gadgeteering, constructing Rube-Goldbergesque devices that were more entertaining than practical. Since he wasn't able to apply this skill in class, he employed it in his second favorite hobby: practical jokes. Soon, he had earned the animosity of the others in his dorm and even some of his teachers.

Slowly, his activities slowly became more deviant. Circumventing security in the administration building, climbing campus buildings and even dabbling in minor pyrotechnics became more interesting than the tame classroom approaches to physics and mathematics. Breaking and entering became easier once he found his way into the school's storm tunnels. By the time he had met other masters of "urban spelunking," he had developed a certain mastery in his craft. If only he hadn't stumbled into the wrong laboratory….

There were two mages in the University, each one looking for a prospective student. The local Son of Ether was reluctant to take on such a troublesome apprentice, but Shawn's second instructor was delighted. It is indeed fortunate that the Scientist does not know about Shawn's extracurricular activities. Shawn has learned a few tricks from a Nephandus, a *barabbi* of an Arabian society of mages known as the Ahl-i-Batin. Though he knows all the proper social protocols of the Sons' society, he also has darker insights into more frightening applications of Forces and Correspondence.

The choice between his two Paths torments Shawn; he avoids making a decision by mucking around in the dark — alone, more often than not. Whatever political obligations Shawn holds to the Chantry pale in comparison to his choice: he supports Hype because the Renegade Faction values the data he gathers in the tunnels. Sooner than Shawn would prefer, the choice between light and darkness will be forced upon him by circumstance….

Image: Shawn literally dresses in the dark, so he doesn't care about his appearance. When you crawl in tunnels underground, it's hard to recognize bright green tennis shoes under layers of muck or see if the stains on your blue jeans match three-year-old T-shirts. The two constants in his appearance are the bicycle lamp he wears mounted to his baseball cap and the backpack he carries with the many electrical devices he uses in his security systems and traps.

Roleplaying Hints: Soul-searching requires a great deal of privacy. You're torn between two choices: will you reject the whisperings of the night, or meet your obligations as a brilliant scientist? Though the companionship of others draws you out occasionally, you retreat when anyone forces you to consider the future.

Quote: *No, no, no, I'm sure it's around here somewhere. I think I could find it more easily if I turned off this light….*

Magnus
Master of Synthesis

Faction: Renegade Cabal
Tradition: Orphan
Nature: Visionary
Demeanor: Avant-Garde
Essence: Primordial
Attributes: Strength 2, Dexterity 2, Stamina 3, Charisma 3, Manipulation 2, Appearance 3, Perception 3, Intelligence 4, Wits 2
Abilities: Alertness 2, Brawl 1, Computer 3, Cosmology 3, Dodge 1, Enigmas 2, Expression (Music) 4, Firearms 3, Medicine 3, Occult 2, Technology (Synthesizers) 4
Backgrounds: Avatar 2, Dream 2, Node 2, Talisman 3
Spheres: Correspondence 2, Spirit 3, Prime 2
Willpower: 7
Arete: 3
Quintessence: 3
Paradox: 4

Background: The cutting edge leads to frightening possibilities. As one of the programmers for a struggling industrial band, Magnus (the artist formerly known as Donald Jefferson) was always attracted to the dark side of techno. As part of his effort to stay ahead of groups like the Electric Hellfire Club and Leather Strip, Magnus' music became increasingly bitter and hostile. Samplings from old horror films, porno films and WW II documentaries resulted in a mix that was just too nasty to be commercially acceptable.

His experimentation in music led him to an intense Awakening during a late-night composition marathon. The devil (his Avatar?) came to him then and promised him power if he used that power to preach a dark message. Writing the

whole thing off as sleep deprivation, Magnus worked his Arts unconsciously, using techno music and gear to focus his minor (but growing) knowledge. His final commercial effort, a retrospective of the history of the Golden Dawn, brought him revelation, opening a temporary gateway into another Realm. As he attained the impossible and transcended the material, he brought on the greatest Paradox backlash of his life.

What he saw scared the hell out of him, and he changed the style of his music almost overnight. The code he created for his last project is hidden away behind layers of computer security. He has desperately tried to take a more New Age approach in his work, mainly because he's terrified of "summoning up that which he cannot put down." Though the others know of his skill, they don't know that he has discovered the code for a gateway to Malfeas, one of the deepest levels of the underworld.

Image: Every day is a performance. Magnus has shaved his head, and has an affinity for jumpsuits and flowing robes. Confidentially, it's a good thing he doesn't get out more with his taste in so-called "fashion." He's got a wide assortment of sunglasses, but he prefers to wear a virtual "viewmaster"-type terminal when he's working. The electrical wiring he has set up under the stage now acts as a focus for his mastery of the Spirit Sphere. Branwyn carries on a bitter rivalry with Magnus, but Miriam, the Chantry's Dreamspeaker, finds his work intriguing. Magnus finds her interruptions to be annoying.

Roleplaying Notes: You know firsthand how dangerous technology is, which makes you even more defensive when Traditional mages criticize your work. Though you're still too cool for words around others, in private you pray for forgiveness for the things you did and the lies you once told. Every once in a while, you hold arguments between your inner devil and your "reborn" self. Although traditional religion is not your way, you seek repentance and an inner peace before it's too late.

Quote: *If no one else will tell you, I will. The old ways are dead. If you do not adapt to the future, you will die.*

Miriam Dunsany

Theatrical Wonder

Faction: Traditional Cabal
Tradition: Dreamspeaker
Nature: Traditionalist
Demeanor: Caregiver
Essence: Primordial
Attributes: Strength 2, Dexterity 2, Stamina 3, Charisma 3, Manipulation 2, Appearance 3, Perception 3, Intelligence 3, Wits 3
Abilities: Alertness 4, Brawl (Tai Chi) 1, Culture 3, Dodge 2, Etiquette 3, Expression (Acting) 4, Intuition 3, Medicine 3, Meditation 4, Occult 3
Backgrounds: Avatar 4, Dream 3, Node 2
Spheres: Life 3, Mind 2, Prime 2, Spirit 3
Willpower: 5

Arete: 3
Quintessence: 6
Paradox: 2

Background: The life of a struggling artist is never easy. Miriam began her career as a performance artist in the '60s, and she never grew up. Floating from one financially unstable theater troupe to another, she has been a part of everything from grassroots rock bands and protest concerts to Renaissance fairs and tribal ceremonies.

Miriam is the peacemaker and the keeper of ceremonies. Although she wants to use more of them to bring the Chantry together, the Renegades find them somewhat ludicrous. To counteract this, she has taken an interest in the practices of the Technomages, and has even offered to incorporate her dancing into one of Magnus' performances. She's very attracted to him, despite the fact that she's 20 years older.

Image: Very personable. She inherently trusts just about anyone, and has a knack for seeing the good qualities in people. Her clothes usually have a world-beat aspect, and she is quite fond of combining her blue jeans and Birkenstocks with fashion ideas from Third World countries. Her hair has slowly turned gray, but her smile is as vivid as it was 30 years ago.

Roleplaying Hints: Why wear a long face? Most people, you know, can't seem to appreciate the miracle of being alive. You do, however, and each day you thank the spirits and the gods for your existence. Honor all things — even darkness has its place. Not to say you're a sap — hell, no! You've just seen enough people try, and fail, to solve their problems with bloodshed.

Quote: *Stop it! Stop fighting, all of you! Can't you see we're all on the same side? Here, let's form a circle.*

Morgan Celeste

Faction: Traditionalist
Tradition: Orphan
Nature: Conformist
Demeanor: Martyr
Essence: Primordial
Attributes: Strength 2, Dexterity 3, Stamina 3, Charisma 3, Manipulation 2, Appearance 3, Perception 3, Intelligence 3, Wits 4
Abilities: Alertness 3, Brawl 1, Dodge 3, Enigmas 3, Firearms 3, Medicine 3, Streetwise (Information) 4, Survival 3
Backgrounds: Avatar 4, Dream 3
Spheres: Mind 1, Prime 1, Spirit 1
Willpower: 5
Arete: 1
Quintessence: 4
Paradox: 2

Background: Poverty has stalked Morgan all her life. When she dropped out of college at the age of 19, she had trouble holding down a minimum-wage job without getting bored out of her mind. Instead, she preferred to spend time with the people in her community. Volunteering at a community shelter was just what she needed. Her usual approach is to get involved in projects when they're starting out, but once they're working, she moves on. Her latest involvements concern a mission a few blocks away from the Pike's Place Market and a Food Not Bombs group that feeds the homeless nearby.

Morgan has barely Awakened, and the dreams (Seekings) she has get worse as her Avatar, which appears as a stern angel with black and empty eyes, loses patience with her. The mission where she works is very religious, but Morgan has never believed in God. Although she's beginning to witness "miracles" around her, she isn't sure who to tell. Her dreams are filled with Christian imagery, but she doesn't feel comfortable turning to the other people at the mission.

Branwyn was able to anticipate Morgan's Awakening, and she has volunteered to be responsible for her until the Chorus can be contacted. There's one more complication, though: Morgan has started to fall in love with Branwyn, and she can't think of a way to tell her. This only adds to her confusion. Although she cares a great deal about the people around her, Morgan is scared by the lack of easy answers in her new life. She's especially concerned with how the activities in Seattle will affect Sleepers. Everything is terribly new and frightening to her, and learning about a extradimensional theater underground naturally hasn't helped.

Image: A quiet girl barely out of her teens, Morgan is soft-spoken but bears a winning smile and a compassionate eye. Her self-esteem is somewhat lacking, but her vulnerability is exceedingly charming. Worrying is a constant condition with Morgan. She's somewhat overweight, her hair is always disheveled, and she frets constantly.

Roleplaying Hints: Your voice is soft and hesitant, and you don't always speak up when you should. You adore Branwyn's sense of style and beauty, and you wish you had half her confidence and looks, which only increases your lack of self-esteem. You go out of your way to be polite to everyone, and you're ready to help anyone in trouble. As you're trying to find your niche as a mage, this new world frightens you, and you're anxious about every move you make.

Quote: *No, I don't think that's a terribly wise thing for you to do. I think if a group of nine-foot — what do you call them, Garou? — went running through downtown, the people there wouldn't take it terribly well.*

Adventures

I don't question our existence
I just question our modern needs
— Pearl Jam (of course), "Garden"

Notable Groups in Seattle

• Benning Aircraft

Benning, the primary employer in the Seattle area, carries a *lot* of clout. It's also almost invisible in its home city. Some say that if a law dies in the Washington legislature, the logging industry didn't like it, but if the law disappears entirely, Benning didn't like it.

The Technocracy doesn't need to control Benning: the Sleepers who work there are already thoroughly conditioned in the principles of corporate oppression. While the corporation demands loyalty and trust from its employees, they're also notorious for dumping considerable numbers of them back into the job market during difficult times. Workers get the frustration of being told of their "empowerment" at the same time their hands are tied by bureaucracy. After years of subtle conditioning, a corporation cast-off has usually sold his independence for a stack of paychecks and the knowledge that he's worked for the "good of the company." The result is a dupe who goes swimming back into the ocean of Sleepers.

The opportunity for infiltration, however, is too good to completely ignore. The Technocracy has set aside a Construct within the corporation. The Syndicate has liberated funding for the "Benning Air and Space Research Center." This base of operations is about 10 minutes' drive from the Sea-Tac airport. The building has a respectable front, including (thanks to the PR Department) a museum of avionics for tourists. Back in the "restricted" areas, the Void Engineers have a major headquarters. Other autonomous "project teams" within Benning include a security team controlled by Iteration X that manages to put in "overtime" off-site and a Quality Management team run by a Gray Suit of the New World Order named Cyril Gosstocks. The three teams despise each other, but thanks to "creative" financing, they have the resources they need to carry out missions "for the good of the company."

• Macrosoft's Virtual Adepts

Macrosoft's headquarters is in the Seattle area; while it's just as powerful and monolithic as Benning, the company handles its world domination with a bit more flair and a lot less crushing of the human spirit. The 12 Virtual Adepts within the establishment are able to sustain sizable paychecks while treasuring their access to valuable equipment. Their hidden clashes with Benning, however, could erupt into a major economic war in a very short time. The constant bickering between Macrosoft and Apple Computers is a ruse to keep the Technocracy off-guard. The two companies both cover a secret society of Cybernauts who do most of their work on the Digital Web.

• The Cult of Quadigsi

"Quadigsi" is a bit of Native American folklore, an entity variously described as a giant snake, a giant octopus or a huge humanoid creature — possibly as tall as a skyscraper—with aspects of both of these creatures. Supposedly, it lives in Puget Sound, where it occasionally rises to have a quick meal before gong back into the deep. There is, of course, no hard evidence for the existence of such a creature. Most scholars believe it to be pure myth, or *possibly* exaggerated tales of whales who wandered into the Sound.

However, there are those who believe otherwise — a small but steadily growing underground cult believes that Quadigsi not only exists, but is the physical manifestation of an otherworldly horror with vast supernatural powers. Led by a charismatic Infernalist sorcerer, the unholy union meets and performs its nefarious rites in a variety of makeshift temples throughout the city, going randomly from site to site to confound anyone who might be observing.

• Liquid Haze

Hollow Ones come and go, but the Haze never fades. This slice of heaven is a candlelit coffee shop that's open from early in the morning to late at night. Refills of drip coffee are a quarter, and the people working there can mix exotic coffees like a bartender mixes drinks (faster than you can say "double-tall half-caff non-fat vanilla latte"). The mix of music is better than what you'll find on the local radio stations. Steady customers include a group of Hollow Ones who usually surround themselves with their Sleeper friends. The latest addition to their clique is Heather Cross, an Euthanatos with a bitter grudge against Rudolfo: because of her Tradition, he won't let her near the Theater. The Haze is a great place to find out what's happening in some of the alternative communities of Seattle.

• The Call of the Wyld

Most Americans don't think of their country as having rainforests, but the Pacific Northwest is one of four such areas in the world. Although the deforestation isn't as massive as the destruction in the Amazon, environmental activists watch the logging industry carefully. Werewolves and their allies constantly fight developers, logging consortiums and tourism companies who encroach on the small areas of unspoiled wilderness left. Most of these Garou are pretty extreme in their hostility toward mankind — they see the Pacific Northwest as their last frontier, and if it should fall, they might as well roll over and wait for the end.

The tales of the Sasquatch (i.e., "Bigfoot") in this area are, as one would expect, actually accounts of encounters with Garou that have been garbled by the strange effects of the

Delirium. The Garou are revered by the Native Americans in this area as "mountain spirits," and a tribe of Children of Gaia had openly mingled with them until the mid-1800s. However, with the popular collection of "Bigfoot" stories in the 20th century, spirits matching the Bigfoot model have begun to manifest. Whether this is a manifestation of consensual reality or a new type of spirit in the Umbra remains to be seen — the spirits rarely hang around.

• The Kindred

Just as the relations between the Garou and the Kindred are fairly amiable in nearby Vancouver, the Anarch Wars of the early '90s that raged across the West Coast have forced the Camarilla to focus on repopulation instead of interfering with the activities of the Garou. As the city's vampires assemble under the watchful eyes of Petrodon, the local Nosferatu Justicar, an increasing number of bloodlines have joined their ranks. The Ravnos in particular are gathering in the city in force, and their Gypsy associates are assisting them. The city's primogen members are anxious to find out why… and the Ravnos, of course, aren't telling.

• Magicians of the Bay

In the nearby city of Renton, another suspicious gathering has occurred. A company curiously named "The Magicians of the Bay" has found their way to unexpected success. Once a small devoted group of gamers working in a basement, they made a miraculous discovery: the invention of a card game called *Magick: The Apocrypha*. Devised by an occult researcher and theologian from nearby Walla Walla, the game has become an unprecedented success. Magicians of the Bay (or "MotB," as its affectionately called) has since developed ties to the Black Dog Game Factory, which draws attention to them from the occasional investigator. They've also blossomed into a large corporation, which leads some to suspect an influence from the Syndicate. The game, however, suggests a Tradition collaboration, and as for its popularity, well…. As part of its rapid growth, it's accumulated a number of employees with mysterious and unusual backgrounds. MotB continues to spread across the world, and the curious speculate on what will result.

Story Ideas

• **The Road to Hell:** Shawn Cornell has disappeared during one of his expeditions. In the lobby of the theater, he's posted a note stating that he's worried that he may have found an opening to a level of the underworld. Magnus can open a gateway to go after him, if the characters choose, but he doesn't know of Shawn's motivations. Shawn has been offered knowledge if he can lead a few unwitting victims into the labyrinth of his Nephandus master. After that, the plan is completely in the hands of the Ahl-i-Batin *barabbi*. Will the players discover Shawn's treachery?

• **Children of the Light:** One of the characters, while visiting a bookstore in Pioneer Square, uncovers a valuable tome. Under the glass of one of the counters is a book on the legend of Quadigsi. The book is "on hold" for another customer, but the owner won't begrudge the mage a chance to look at it. Tales of horror are interspersed with dark demi-Hermetic rites. Just as the mage has a chance to finish looking at the book, another customer arrives and purchases it. The mage and the purchaser exchange a brief glance. How far will the characters go to find out more about the Cult of Quadigsi?

• **Cat with a :-)** : Cheshire (the sample character from the **Mage** rulebook) has some startling news for the characters' cabal. He appears on a television set in front of one of the mages, and reveals that he's found out about a recent Technocracy raid on the Theater! All of the performers are missing, and only Cheshire has clues as to their whereabouts. Have any of them fallen into the clutches of the NWO, or are they merely hiding somewhere else? How much damage control can the characters do? The grinning Cat's in a position to bargain now....

• **Errant Child:** Morgan is extremely concerned about a member of her "flock." A 12-year-old girl who lives on the streets of downtown Seattle is starting to run packages for a minor drug syndicate downtown. She doesn't want to take on this problem alone, so Hype has offer to help the characters investigate. Unfortunately, Hype botches his part of the investigation; he'll owe the characters big-time if they can save his ass... and his reputation.

• **Deadly Politics:** Branwyn has gone a little too far. She's gained a brief alliance with Shawn by offering to help him in his efforts. By manipulating a few threads of her loom, she can predict a few permutations of the maze of tunnels over the next few days. The fact that she's showing great sympathy towards him — and meeting with him in the maze after hours — is working to her advantage. The characters stumble upon one of her "amorous" encounters. What will they do with the knowledge? Does Branwyn want to break Shawn's heart, or is there the possibility of another outcome?

• **Rave Against the Dying of the Light**: A group of changelings have arrived from San Francisco. They've set up a Renaissance fair outside of town, and Branwyn is delighted to attend. She invites the characters to accompany her as her "escorts," which is just as well, since the local Marauders were also planning on being there! The festivities quickly get out of hand. The characters discover that the Marauders want to use this Glamourous event as a chance to summon a mythic beastie. Can the characters stop them without revealing what's really going on to the Sleepers?

• **Jealousy Kills:** Rudolfo has always been an even-tempered man, but when he finds out about the budding romance between Lisa Yokahama, his Hermetic apprentice, and Hyperion, the Renegade, he becomes furious. He's very protective of his charge, and he forbids to let Hyperion continue to see her unless he can "prove his worth." He challenges him to a certámen duel. Is Rudolfo really as good as he used to be? Is Hyperion in danger? The anger boils to a fever pitch as Branwyn makes an overt display of supporting the Chantry leader as she maneuvers to eliminate her rivals. When rivalries go this deep, sometimes it takes someone objective to solve the problem....

Chapter Three: Storyteller Goodies

Dr. Romain Guy seldom took his work home, but tonight he sat in his makeshift basement laboratory puzzling over the data his research director had given him for the weekend.

The soft thud of tennis shoes on carpeted stairs tore his attention away from the computer screen. Romain looked up in annoyance. "Collette, how many times do I have to tell you…" He stopped when he saw his small daughter standing there, a mass of blood-covered fur in her arms, tears running down her cheeks.

"Papa, someone hit Bianca…" Collette dissolved into sobs when Romain came over and took the cat from her.

"Go outside and play," he said softly, running a hand through her blonde curls. "Go on."

Wordlessly, she obeyed. Romain took the dying cat, placed her on his work bench and thought a moment. He despised the infrequent meetings between his work and his personal life, but in Collette's world, Bianca was far more important than genome-mapping reality deviants. He pulled out a pair of rubber gloves, picked up a scalpel and went to work.

The following tools may be considered Storyteller secrets. Although the final truth behind your chronicle depends on each invidual troupe, the magicks and agendas given in this chapter might ruin some of the mystery behind **Mage**'s scenes. If nothing else, this data should not be common knowledge, especially among young mages.

Obviously, players will buy and read this supplement. Storytellers, then, may wish to modify, alter or ignore the details of this chapter — or at least lead their players to believe that they have…. Ultimately, as always, the best secrets in your chronicle are the ones you make yourself.

Let me call you sweetheart,
Then crush it in your chest and dine.
— Splinters, "Be My Halloween"

Tradition mages got their goodies in Chapter One. The following rotes, Effects and procedures give you some idea of the magick their rivals practice, and may be used for quick reference when you need a spell to throw at your players' characters. The **Technocracy:** sourcebooks and **The Book of Madness** have other useful magicks and sample characters.

Corrupter Magick

Truth does not do as much good in the world as the semblance of truth does evil.

— La Rochefoucauld, *Maxims 64* (1665)

Willworkers in **Mage** chronicles face many antagonists who represent different kinds of corruption. Technomancers are consumed with pride, power and their misguided desire to protect Sleepers from mythic reality. Rival Tradition mages sometimes show intolerance or even insanity, the corruption of self-righteousness. Marauders represent the corruption of the mind itself, and of unrestrained magickal power.

The Nephandi, however, illustrate the clearest examples of corruption. Drawn into evil by Paths of pride, despair, cruelty, obsession and — above all — doubt, the Fallen Ones embody the most dangerous corruption, that of the spirit. This peril works subtly, playing on the desires and guilt felt by every human being, whether Sleeper or Awakened. Each of us is vulnerable to the call of the Corrupt Ones.

Nephandus mages, though they usually command only minor magick, compensate with ruthless cunning. They present tremendous threats to inexperienced Tradition mages, who are often burdened with moral conflicts over proper use of their magick, and to powerful wizards, whose pride rises with their abilities. Moral conflict is the Fallen One's ecological niche: a young Akashic Brother who wants a charming Cultist of Ecstacy to join her cabal; a Chorus mage intent on converting "pagans"; a Euthanatos, threatened by Syndicate blackmail, who feels her only chance to protect her cabal lies in a pact with dark forces — all these are the puppets that a Nephandus dances on her strings.

Most Nephandi invert common magickal styles to work their Arts, or focus them through symbols and acts that most people (including themselves) consider black magic — brutal sacrifices, prayers to dark gods, induced insanity, torture, desecration, slavery, possession, etc. *Barabbi*

often pervert the style they once used, or expand it to a darker extreme (using a computer to spread viruses, for example, or going from peyote to crack). Destructive elements — especially fire, ice and polluted water — are common foci, as are bodily fluids, sewage, trash or even radiation. Although most Labrynths share common rituals, most Nephandi prefer the personal approach to magick styles.

Mindscreen (• Mind)

Among the first Effects a Nephandus mage learns, this simple rote disguises her perfidious thoughts from prying Mind Effects. She cannot, however, pass for a Sleeper; this requires more advanced Mind magick that induces misconceptions in the snooping mage's mind.

[The Nephandus makes an Effect roll to resist the unwanted Mind Effect. Each success he rolls subtracts one success from his opponent. If the Nephandus scores more successes than his rival, he may control the impression the opponent receives. This is coincidental magick.]

What Did You Say? (•• Correspondence, •• Mind)

The Nephandi work their corruption one mage at a time. A Fallen One chooses a victim and works on him with spider-like patience, first inducing anxiety and vulnerability, then separating him from friends, and finally attacking or seducing him. This rote figures early in the fateful process.

Nephandi can make their targets mishear the most ordinary conversation as vaguely ominous, insulting or meaningless. For example, "Have another drink, will you?" becomes "Having too much to drink, are you?" Over a long period (sometimes over the course of one dinner party), this encourages alienation, nervousness and suspicion in the prey. The rote works best when the mage is eavesdropping on a (distorted) conversation that he cannot join without breaching etiquette.

[The number of successes on the Effect roll must match or exceed the victim's Perception rating. A botch means the would-be victim becomes aware of the manipulation. A simple Mind 2 variation can affect anyone in the mystick's close proxcimity.]

Buzz (•• Prime)

Having persuaded his target that he's a Sleeper, a corrupter may enchant her (figuratively speaking) with charming conversation, subtle praise, soulful looks and other signals of attraction. He also covertly increases the flow of Quintessence through the target's Life Pattern, giving her a mild, barely noticeable pleasure. "Around him, things just seem more *real*," a victim may say early in their acquaintance.

Mages of different Traditions have different reactions to this Effect. A Cultist of Ecstacy recognizes it at once and dismisses it as small potatoes, whereas a naive Akashic Brother might mistake it for a sign on the way to enlightenment.

[This Effect works as the Prime 2 magick **Rubbing of the Bones**, but it stimulates instead of pains. Only one success is necessary. The target's small injuries may heal more quickly, or the Storyteller may reduce the difficulty of some magick rolls. The target is not usually aware of the Effect unless the roll is botched. The Storyteller may grant the target a Perception + Awareness roll to detect the Quintessence increase, although this does not identify the Effect's source. If she becomes aware of the Effect, she can spend a point of stored Quintessence to smooth the flow and cancel the Effect.]

Frame Up (••• Matter, •• Mind)

Cunning, misdirection, connivance: these are the tools of the Nephandi. This Effect fabricates a convincing illusion that leaves real aftereffects, such as broken furniture or lipstick on a cheek. With Life 3 instead of Matter 3, the illusion can include such consequences as a burning cheek from a slap, minor aches, symptoms of pregnancy, etc.

Nephandi use this to create incriminating sights among a victim's friends and acquaintances in order to alienate them. They might see the victim make a clumsy seduction attempt, scream imprecations or "reveal" false secrets about himself.

[Viewers may resist the illusion with Willpower or countermagick if they have some reason to doubt it. If the illusion is skillful, however, they remain unaware of the Effect. The number of successes determines the complexity and realism of the illusion: three or more successes indicates a convincing sight.

[Variations of this rote are common. Prime 2 may be added to create items that did not already exist, while Forces 2/ Correspondence 2 can alter videotape images (see the **Point-to-Point Narrow-Band Transmission** rote in Chapter One). With a lot of time, patience, Matter 2 and a few dots in Technology, the Fallen One can create brand-new videotapes of damning but fictional events — a theft, vandalism, murder, etc.]

Loving Scar (••• Life, •• Spirit)

This Effect scars the target. The method of creating the scar varies with each Nephandus, but the scar is most effective when applied in the most intimate circumstances with the willing cooperation of the victim. Depending on the means, this magick may well be coincidental. The scar does no damage, but it cannot be healed except with Life 4 magick.

After the scarring, the victim attracts minor Umbrood spirits that spy on or torment him. The spirits do no damage — no lasting damage, at any rate — but they create nuisances as well as the victim's senses and alienate him from his companions. Suppose that a Son of Ether, scarred by this Effect, attracts an Epiphling, this one a minor embodiment of Truth; suppose further that the Umbrood announces the

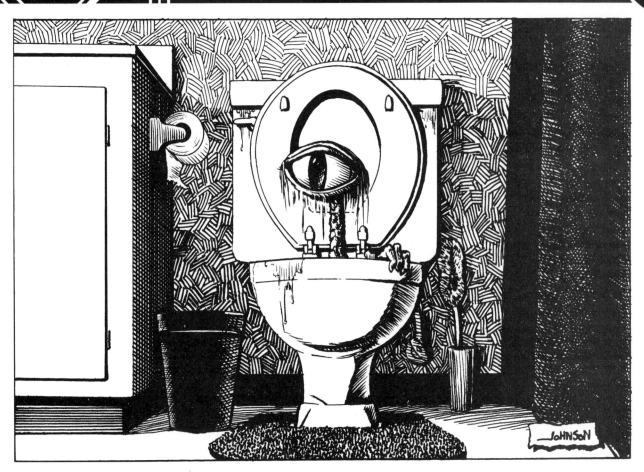

most guarded passwords of the Etherite's companion Virtual Adept during a tense confrontation with Men in Black. The Adept and her companions, if they're aware of the scar at all, will strongly suggest that the Etherite victim go off on a private retreat until the scar heals.

[The number of successes on the Effect roll determines how long the Effect lasts. Most casters try to make it permanant. The scar attracts spirits of low (Minion) power, such as Gafflings.]

Blindside (•••• Correspondence, •• Matter)

After a Fallen One isolates and terrorizes her victim, she strikes from surprise. This rote lets the Nephandus attack a target physically from a completely unexpected direction — by reaching through the drain of a bathroom sink (or, worse, the toilet bowl); sending gas attacks through a telephone handset; or, for theatrical effect, flooding a phone booth while the target makes a call. The damage itself is minor for the magick required. The Corrupted One desires instead to make the target wary, jumpy and prone to error.

[The attack requires at least two successes, and inflicts one Health Level of normal damage for each success beyond the second. At the Storyteller's discretion, the target may receive a Perception + Awareness roll to detect the attack (difficulty 8).]

Exalted Desire (•••• Life, •• Mind, •• Prime)

This subtle Effect gives its target an unusual high while experiencing some favored pleasure. Over time, it can make any pleasant behavior addictive. The Nephandi use it to increase their prey's vulnerability to temptation. The roster of Ecstacy Cultists corrupted by this rote makes a long, sad recitation.

[Only one success is necessary to create the Effect — thus its insidiousness. The victim may roll Intelligence + Awareness or spend a point of Willpower to resist, but usually does not wish to. Successes accumulate with repeated use. When the cumulative successes exceed the victim's Willpower rating, she can be considered addicted to the pleasure, and must roll Intelligence + Awareness or spend Willpower to avoid succumbing whenever the opportunity presents itself. Getting free of the addiction requires diligent effort, and can become the subject of a story or even an entire chronicle.]

Mad Magick

It's worse than wicked, my dear, it's vulgar.
— *Punch Almanac (1876)*

Whereas the Nephandi embody a seductive corruption, Marauders represent the other narrative extreme: the repellent and frightening corruption of unrestrained power, of dynamism unchecked — "There but for the grace of God go I," as it were. Tradition mages may envy the Mad Ones' immunity to Paradox effects, but most fear the Wyld madness and its disconnection to others' reality.

Marauders do not learn their magick by rote; each one creates different Effects. Tradition mages simply affix names retroactively to Effects they see cast by individual Marauders. Episodes of Chaos Mage activity are typically brief and crazed, and exact observations are difficult. The spectacularly vulgar nature of chaos magick, however, offsets this problem somewhat.

Mad magick styles are unique; each Marauder casts his Arts through means as individual as his madness. Some use elaborate rites, while others play games, invent poetry or seem to shrug mystick muscles and have things simply *happen*. The following Effects are only some notable examples of the crafts of insanity.

That Rascal Puff (••• Life, ••• Forces, •• Prime)

The Virtual Master Dante likes to tell stories of a solitary Marauder he encountered while infiltrating the Syndicate data compiling firm AlphaFax. According to the Adept, "that rascal Puff" stepped from nowhere during Dante's late-night unauthorized tour of the facilities. Going from room to room, the Maruader turned the machines in each office on with a simple gesture while Dante watched from hiding. Once all the computers were on and networklinked, the Mad One (who Dante describes as having scaly gray skin and sharp teeth and claws) breathed a sudden fire cloud on one terminal, causing every computer on the network to explode. The sudden blast expanded into a Paradox backlash which demolished everything in the Marauder's room. When the smoke cleared, Dante was alone. "Whether the bastard survived that or not," Dante says, "I don't know, but I'm betting he did."

[It's very likely that the Marauder had both Computer Knowledge and the passwords for the network. To link all the computers without such knowledge would demand an extended Wits + Computer roll (difficulty 7-10, depending on the system's complexity) or Correspondence 2 and a few dots in Computer (see "Hacking," **Mage Second Edition**, pp. 244-245). Once the system is linked, the Forces/ Prime blast sends a shock throughout the link, damaging any computer tied to the system.

[Life magick allows the Marauder to breathe fire; a mage could try the disruption Effect without doing so, and could, of course, breathe fire without destroying an office network. This Effect inflicts typical Forces damage.]

Babel (•••• Mind)

An unmentioned episode in the history of the Lodge of the Gray Squirrel (see **The Book of Chantries**) concerns a mage named Mary Tomesha, an Orphan of Mohave (Mojave) and Anglo descent.

In 1960, the Chantry recruited Tomesha from the Colorado River Reservation in Arizona. Though she took to her studies well, Tomesha seemed withdrawn and homesick. No one knows when she slipped into Quiet, but one day three years later, every member of the lodge imperceptibly began speaking the Mohave language, Yuman. They understood one another perfectly; no one realized the change until they emerged from the Horizon Realm and found outsiders unintelligible. Investigating, they found that Mary Tomesha believed she had returned home. If she had developed greater skill in the Sphere of Matter, she would have transformed the Lodge into a copy of the reservation.

Chantry leader Tom Smithson ("Laughing Eagle") confined Tomesha in a pastoral region of the Horizon Realm. Some years later, Tomesha vanished, and her whereabouts are unknown.

[The number of successes determines the duration and scope of the Effect — in most cases, one person per success. In the absence of obvious evidence, those affected by the rote receive a Wits + Awareness roll (difficulty 8) to realize that they are speaking a different language.]

Back to the Earth (•••• Matter, ••• Life, •• Prime)

Former Greenpeace member, monkey-wrencher and eco-warrior, Verbena mage Carl Matthew Landless snapped during an anti-logging protest in the Pacific Northwest. His first few Effects, all explosions, sent Sleeper witnesses running. Only a coven of Verbena (Landless' erstwhile companions), saw Landless convert several bulldozers into tree sculptures. "They looked like topiary shrubs," Heasha Morningshade said later. "They were beautiful, until Paradox spirits moved in and consumed them." Landless escaped while the coven fought the spirits, and his current whereabouts are unknown.

[The number of successes governs how much inorganic material can be converted to living wood. A bulldozer requires four successes.]

Temple Pillars (•••• Forces, ••• Matter, •• Prime)

Early July, 1994: Mercenary forces fighting in the disputed Aozou Strip between Libya and Chad were shocked when the desert shook and pillars of stone rose slowly from the sand. Four lines of sandstone columns, as big as the ruined pillars of Luxor in Egypt, marked off the battlefield. Gunfire could not damage them. When the columns had grown to 30 feet tall, a grinning Persian magus (later identified as an old Batini who had gone mad during their war with the Technocracy) appeared atop each one; gunfire could not damage him either.

Lightning crackled around the mystick as he shouted, "What a barbaric waste! Is this any kind of occupation for civilized people? Throw down your weapons, and walk with me into a better life!" The mercenaries, who were not stupid, reluctantly threw down their weapons and followed the Marauder. Using Correspondence magick, he led them across a hundred yards of desert into Ethiopia's desolate coastal province of Eritrea, 1100 miles to the southeast.

In a village emptied by famine some years before, the mad Batini halted the men and gestured broadly at the empty huts. "Rebuild these humble shacks. Let a new city of peace spring up in this war-torn province." The men asked where they would get supplies, food and citizens. With an air of annoyance, the Mad One said, "Right, right, I'll take care of that, just a moment." He vanished, but something evidently distracted him, for he never returned. Many of the mercenaries died of thirst before they reached an inhabited town, and the Ethiopian government imprisoned the rest as illegal aliens.

[The Effect raises a structure, creating it from ground material as it rises. Matter reshapes the ambient material, Prime fixes the new Pattern, and Forces raises the reshaped structure telekinetically.

[Three successes are required on an extended roll to raise a structure the size of a small house. Each additional success adds 500 square feet to its size. Ordinarily the Effect requires one day, but the mage can spend two additional successes to reduce the time to one scene, or four extra successes to reduce it to one turn.

[The Correspondence 4 Effect **Polyappearance** produces the duplicates of the mage.]

Temple Gongs (•••• Forces, •••• Matter, •••• Mind, ••• Life, •• Prime)

July 27, 1992: At the Kamakura beach resort south of Yokohama, Japan, Arlan "The Smiler" Nattick walked through a medieval Zen Buddhist temple, a popular tourist site. As he passed the temple gongs, they rang loudly. Tourists who heard the ringing threw away their video cameras, fell to their knees and began droning a Buddhist chant, the *Vatthupama-sutta* or "Parable of the Piece of Cloth." While they chanted, their clothing changed to the bright orange robes of Buddhist monks and their hair fell out.

The new monks walked in a line through Kamakura, with Nattick following at a distance, and begged from passersby, who freely handed over their money, watches, jewelry and clothing. At this point a cabal of Akashic Brothers showed up and demanded an explanation from Nattick, who replied, "I just wondered if Buddhism really worked." Before the Akashics could determine what Nattick meant, or whether his Effect had satisfied his curiosity, a host of Paradox spirits showed up. In the resulting confusion, Nattick casually departed.

[The Forces Sphere creates the gong sounds, Matter and Life physically transform the people, and Mind brainwashes them. Each three successes changes two people; extended rolls convert a crowd. Prime 2 is needed to make the transformation last beyond the Effect's usual duration.]

Nuzzlings (••••• Prime, ••• Matter, ••• Spirit)

Edith Nussbaum, a solitary and disgruntled postal worker in Overland Park, Kansas, went mad within nine seconds of Awakening. She left the Postal Service without killing anyone — that day, anyway — and retreated to her lonely studio apartment, where over three sleepless months she developed a twisted but profound magickal skill.

Having befriended a multitude of Umbrood, Nussbaum headed to the post office. As she walked, she left a wake of animated objects: smiling street lamps, affectionate mailboxes, fireplugs that sang, "Let me be your friend," and sidewalks that extruded caressing hands. At the post office Nussbaum stared at the concrete floor, and tentacles erupted and grasped her former supervisors. The tendrils sucked the life energy from their victims, then rushed to hug the Marauder. She greeted them lovingly, and in the joy of the moment they absentmindedly sucked the life from her too.

[The Effect creates a zone of Spirit-animated objects centered on the mage. The number of successes rolled determines how wide the zone is. One success means arm's length; three, a few yards; and five, a city block. Objects in the zone drain Quintessence as the Prime 5 Effect **Alter Flow**.

[The spirit manifestations are guided by the (often subconscious) desires of the Marauder. They rarely last more than a scene.]

Technocracy Procedures

Mathematics takes us still further from what is human, into the region of absolute necessity, to which not only the actual world, but every possible world, must conform.

— Bertrand Russell, *The Study of Mathematics*

The Technocratic Union frowns upon needless magick use; nevertheless, they are mages in their own right, evn if their Arts work within a somewhat static paradigm. Technocracy magick always requires a focus, and creating an Effect typically takes more time than a Tradition mage needs. Many Technomancer Effects, however, are often coincidental, which gives them an edge in survivability if not spontenaity. (See **Mage Second Edition**: "Foci," pp. 181-184; "Magickal Geography and Influence," pp. 184-186; and "Technomagick," pg. 68 for details.)

Sustenance Pill (••• Life, •• Prime)

Decades ago, Progenitor Pharmacopeists developed a pill to assist the Void Engineers in their space travels. The capsule frees the mage from the need for food, sleep and (over long usage) elimination. The Sons of Ether and Virtual Adepts like these pills, popularly known as "evergreens," but most other Traditions disdain them.

[The number of successes rolled determines how many days the mage may go without food or sleep. A botch inflicts one Health Level of damage, which can disable or kill a target who's already injured.]

Remote Piloting Override (••• Forces, •• Prime, • Matter)

Iteration X Time-Motion Managers are testing an experimental hand-held console that senses and interferes with the electronic components in a mundane (Sleeper-made) motor vehicle. By twisting the console's dials, the Technomancer can remotely take over the vehicle, guiding it or stopping it as he wishes. ("Goodbye, Mr. Bond!") The Effect works poorly against magickal vehicles, which Iteration X doesn't completely understand — cars controlled by Virtual Adept computers, Sons of Ether contraptions and rival Conventions' limousines.

[The Technocrat rolls his Arete against a Strength + Drive roll by the driver or pilot of the target vehicle, difficulty 7. If the Technocrat rolls more successes, he controls the vehicle for that turn.]

Crocodile Blood (•••• Life, •• Matter)

This Effect lets a Progenitor Genegineer alter the hemoglobin in his own blood so that carbon dioxide binds to it, creating bicarbonate ions that cause the hemoglobin to release more oxygen. Consequently, he can hold his breath for an hour or more when calm, or for several minutes of constant activity. The focus is a lengthy blood-replacement technique in gender conditions, making the rote coincidental.

[The number of successes determines the Effect's duration in hours (calm immobility) or minutes (furious action). A botch means the mage must surface immediately or begin to drown. With Prime 2, the Progenitor can create this Effect for others.]

Re-education Mode (•••• Mind, ••• Time, •• Prime)

This New World Order procedure uses the same approach as the Cult of Ecstacy rote **The Moment That Stretches** (Chapter One), but against an unwilling victim. The dilation of the time sense causes the paralyzed victim to experience hours or days of mental boredom in a few moments of physical time. Agents use this Effect to drive a victim crazy with boredom and sensory deprivation, or to indoctrinate her with endless repetitious messages only she can hear. In some cases, the Effect stretches the victim's subjective time to a week or more — easily long enough to break most wills. The Technocracy often uses this procedure in conjunction with drugs or magickal machines called Sleepteachers (see **Technocracy: NWO**).

[The number of successes on the Effect roll is the number of successes the victim needs on an Intelligence + Meditation roll to break free of the procedure. The victim receives one roll per subjective "hour," but each attempted roll costs a Willpower point, and successes are not cumulative. The Willpower point spent to make the roll does not grant an automatic success; however, the victim can spend additional Willpower points on the same roll to get automatic successes.]

[If the victim cannot break free of the procedure before running out of Willpower, she may receive a post-hypnotic command at the Storyteller's discretion, releasing her from the Effect. Her Mental attributes temporarily drop to one each, and she falls unconscious and remains nonfunctional until she regains at least a point of Willpower. Unless some event reminds her of the command, she will not rember it upon awakening.

[When resisting a post-hypnotic command, the victim uses the same difficulty number and ability roll, but need not spend a Willpower point to make resistance rolls. When the victim scores five cumulative successes, she has broken the post-hypnotic command.]

Nearest and Dearest (••• Mind, •• Correspondence, •• Time)

This insidious procedure helps Syndicate Enforcers convince a victim to do their will. A Syndicate goon hugs his victim, kisses him lightly on both cheeks and either looks through his wallet, performs a background check or simply lets him know, "I've been askin' questions about you, and I know where you live." In this way, the goon identifies and locates anyone that the victim loves or has ever loved, including all living relatives and close friends.

[The victim may resist the Effect roll with Wits + Subterfuge or with Mind countermagick. The Effect grants the caster the name and image of the victim's closest friend or loved one if the Syndicate agent gains at least one success; more successes reveal more names and locations.]

Liftoff (•••• Forces, •••• Matter, •• Prime)

Common opinion considers this one of the most insanely vulgar Effects in history. Invented by the Void Engineers 40 years ago, it makes any flying vehicle spaceworthy. An additional Spirit 4 Effect can carry the vehicle into the Umbra.

The procedure is incredibly Paradox-prone for anything short of a rocket; the details are carefully guarded by the Void Engineers. The Syndicate and New World Order have diligently spread news stories of advances in materials and fuels, making the procedure gradually less unlikely in Sleeper society. In the long term, the Engineers hope to introduce a spacegoing automobile without fear of Paradox.

[The Effect requires seven cumulative successes to reach low Earth orbit and seven more to break the orbit (either to return to Earth or to enter the Deep Umbra). A botch at any point has catastrophic consequences that are left to the Storyteller's imagination. The **Sons of Ether** Tradtion book Appendix lists the rules for Horizon-breaking.]

Storyteller Hints for The Ascension War

No feet to fall
You need no ground
Allowed to glide right through the sun
Released from circles guarded tight
Now we all are chosen ones
— Indigo Girls, "Secure Yourself"

The Ascension War is not a clash of armies or ideologies. It's a battle of souls by souls, and reality is the battleground. The antagonists' agendas and politics, therefore, are as useful to the Storyteller as any list of combat Traits.

It's easy to get lost among the factions of the shadow war. This section offers some clues about the roles and intents of the various groups. Obviously, certain individuals within these groups will deviate from the party line, but the suggestions below should prove helpful. These are not concrete scripts; consider them roleplaying notes for the factions as a whole, like the stereotypes and quotes in the "Traditions" section.

It's really important to remember that True Mages are a rare breed; some may command almost godlike power, but only a handful exist in the world. Estimates of living mysticks (compiled, no doubt, by the Technocracy) range from as low as 2,000 to as high as 10,000 worldwide, including mad Orphans and Horizon Realm dwellers. No one can account for the Nephandi and Marauders beyond the Horizon, but surely only the fittest can survive out there. Even the most generous estimates conclude that most of these willworkers attain only minor powers before either reality or attrition send them back into the Wheel of Creation. Given such small numbers, the direct influence mysticks have upon a mortal world of billions is often slight. Their *indirect* influence is another matter; by pulling at reality's threads, mages keep the Tapestry as a whole from becoming too constricting. The Sleepers take up the slack.

Purposes and Agendas

Each group has a *purpose* or two; think of these as Demeanors (see **Mage Second Edition**, Chapter Six). The *agenda* corresponds somewhat to a Nature; these agendas can give you an insight into that group's general view of Ascension. No crowd is perfect, either; each group has a weakness that wise foes can exploit. With these suggestions, you can get a rough handle on how the group (or characters within that group) will act — or react.

The Traditions

The Mystick Traditions walk a tightrope of control. More than any of their rivals, these mages are subject to doubt or corruption. While the more extreme factions occupy a philosophical niche, the Traditions try to balance between the poles, seeking a personal Ascension over an external one. Hence, it's easier for them to fall from grace into temptation, pride or despair. Their quest against this fall makes Tradition mages more heroic than their peers. Despite their failings, these mystick rebels fight — and prevail — over disconcerting odds.

Within the mortal world, various mysticks exert personal influence. As a whole, however, the Traditions do not pull mortal strings — they let their teachings and examples reach out through events. Once in a while, some group will take a strong role — the Virtual Adepts are directly responsible for the information superhighway, and the Cult of Ecstasy has many allies and agents in the music business — but for the most part, the Traditions are too internally divided to control mortal affairs. And too principled, generally, to seize the reins and command the Sleepers outright.

The Council lacks the Technocrats' unity, but their flexibility ensures their survival. Unlike the Technocracy, this faction's internal rivalries allow their cabals to bend, not break, under stress. Each Tradition has an area where they excel if the shooting starts. They can, however, switch roles much more easily than their static counterparts. Despite their underdog status, the mysticks' romance holds a loyal place in the Sleepers' hearts. Though out-gunned for now, the Council's fortunes are rising.

• The **Akashic Brotherhood** seeks perfection in harmony. Their tool is discipline, which they've refined into a devastating weapon. In open combat, these mages are shock troops — their martial prowess is second to none. Their agenda, however, is complex in its simplicity: to master one's self, and through that, to inspire others. Discipline can be their failing as well — Akashics often crack if their mastery falters.

• **Celestial Chorus** mages minister to humanity; their Ascension is the salvation of the Earth through unity. In this way, some are easily seduced by Technomancers who appeal to their noble purpose. Their greatest strength is their connection to the Sleepers — no other Tradition has such a dedicated base. As defenders of the faith, Choristers counter overt evil with purifying magicks.

• Like the Chorus, the **Cult of Ecstasy** favors changing hearts over ripping them out. This Tradition's ties in the mortal community also run deep, although their anarchistic ideals make them a lot of enemies. When forced to fight, they often distort Time and perception around their targets, averting harm rather than causing it.

• **Dreamspeakers** find strength in the primal connection between the spirit and material worlds. Their agenda is to bridge the gap and let humanity regain its spiritual ties. When they call upon Otherworldly allies, these mages can literally raise hell. Unfortunately, they tend towards tunnel-vision, and get easily distracted by threats to nature's balance and their peoples' well-being.

• **Euthanatos** are silent killers. They don't shoot first and ask questions later; they ask their questions — and get answers — before you even see them coming. When killing is unnecessary, they often teach Sleepers how to appreciate life. Unfortunately, they can be misled; the urge to kill can overpower even the strongest discipline.

• The **Order of Hermes** seeks perfection of the self through perfection of the Art. Their complex rituals require extensive learning and intelligence. When not educating their peers, these mages make excellent tacticians and wield heavy firepower. Their ties to the Sleeper community, though powerful, are slight. This isolation breeds hubris like a petrie dish. Hermetic mages are those most likely to fall to pride.

• The maniacal **Sons of Ether** find strength in their eccentricity, but it makes them hard to take seriously, too. Their Ascension ideal is to take possibility as far as it will go — with style and common decency, of course. Like the Hermetics, the Sons lack the social skills to integrate their vision with common reality; thus, they get rejected and sometimes turn their power against their rivals.

• With the growing New Age movement, **Verbena** mages tap into a whole subculture that feeds their vision. In their quest to unite the sacred and the carnal, these mages seek Ascension inside and help others do the same. This self-searching often leads to self-righteousness; this Tradition is noted for its arrogance. In combat, Verbena wield the forces of life and nature like sabers — swiftly, directly and deadly.

• **Virtual Adepts** are the Council's ace-in-the-hole — and they know it. Their mastery of technology and neo-arcane thought-patterns baffle Tradition and Technomancer alike, which comes in handy in battle. While other mages draw enemy fire, the Adepts hum in behind and…. This Tradition's influence in the modern world is second to none. Their smart-ass reputation, however, makes it hard for them to find friends even when they need them, and their materialistic ways make them easy to seduce. Adept Ascension often involves unity with the Net — transcendence from flesh to information.

• Although the **Hollow Ones** embrace a dark Ascension, their ironic vitality may breathe some much-needed change into the Traditions' corridors. Their anarchistic streak makes any form of unity unlikely, although circumstances may bring them together more than most of them may prefer someday. Until then, they remain a "Tradition" only in the most general sense, and have no formal place within the Council.

Within their personal groups, Hollow Ones tend to be quite loyal; only a select few, they feel, truly understand the shit they've had to take. These Orphans are bootstrap mages — they come into their powers alone and make the best of it with little help. This self-reliance becomes their ideal, though even they refuse to see it. Most of them prefer to avoid a fight, but when backed into corners, they are wickedly unpredictable.

The Technocracy

The Technocratic Union's declared goal is to create a safe reality where random elements are purged and everyone works toward a common purpose under the Conventions' benevolent leadership. Their agenda, however, is a fragmented thing; each Convention has a slightly different take on Ascension, and secretly wishes to control the others. This hamstrings the unity that makes them strong.

To outsiders, the Technocracy is a monolith, ever-present and all-controlling. Because they cloak their magicks in natural laws (both inherent and invented), all but the grossest of their actions are coincidental. This gives them a nasty edge in conflicts with mysticks whose view of reality is more flexible than reality's currents will accept. Although they exert less command over more primal lands and cultures, the Technocrats have the modern world thoroughly in hand.

To the Traditions, the Conventions are everywhere. The truth behind this belief is largely left to the individual Storyteller; despite their seeming omniscience, however, the Technocracy is more show than substance. Many of their most effective techniques involve manipulation and psychological warfare. These strategies make the Technocrats appear more substantial than they actually are.

This faction's vaunted unity is likewise fragile. Although they work effectively together, the Conventions plot against each other when backs are turned. These intrigues are *very* covert; severe penalties greet the Technocrat whose plotting is exposed — especially if it gave some other faction an edge.

The Inner Circle meets in various Horizon Realms; these revolving sites reflect the Conventions' paranoia and security precautions. In some cases, access and information about such meetings may be denied to Technocrats who fall out of favor. Only select representatives from each Convention ever receive an invitation to attend the Inner Circle's gatherings. Although we can assume that such meetings are

heavily guarded, the means remain a mystery — a large regular Symposium would pose security risks. Would-be infiltrators, therefore, could assume that the Inner Circle members are extraordinarily powerful in their own right.

Each Convention has a twofold purpose. The first is the group's day-to-day influence on Sleepers, while the other guides their military function. The agendas reflect the Conventions' ideals — and their intrigues.

• The **NWO's** prime function is indoctrination and infiltration. While their historical divisions write (or re-write) history, intelligence agencies gather information for later use. Their wartime purpose entails conversion, coercion and subtle intimidation. Their agenda is the eventual control of "truth"; under one truth, they hope to unite all humanity.

• **Iteration X** strives for clockwork perfection. Within the Union, they monitor efficiency and update the Timetable which guides the Conventions' actions. On the battlefield, they form the mailed fist of the Technocracy. When brute force is the best response, the Inner Circle sends in Iteration X. The Convention's agenda involves unity with the Machine, a transcendental melding of imperfect opposites.

• The **Syndicate** controls the purse-strings. Their subtle purpose is the regulation of trade and the Sleepers' dependency on it. Their fellow Conventions must likewise win the Syndicate's approval for budgets and research grants. This, of course, leads to lots of politicking. On a more brutal front, the Syndicate's "hard men" lean on those who resist or expose their financial dealings and their progress toward a cashless society. The lowest echelons of their criminal divisions also collect funds and favors from the vice trades, money which goes to fund the other Conventions. Their ideal is command of all trade — perfect regulation screens out random equations. This includes their fellow Technocrats.

• **Progenitor** scientists perform research into the possibilities of the flesh. While seeking organic perfection, they also create tools for the Masses' sedation. A calm child is a happy child, after all. In combat, they employ bizarre creatures, clones and biological weapons. While Iteration X seeks to become one with the Machine, these physicians seek to perfect biological life. Along the way, they indulge in experiments that rival the maddest Marauders for vulgarity. But then, a true scientist must take risks....

• Since their inception, the **Void Engineers** have explored and mapped the unknown. While they usually concentrate on outer space, Engineer Methodologies also travel into the deep seas, inner earth and virtual reality (their mastery of the spirit worlds is a closely-guarded secret). Their wartime purpose is to safeguard these frontiers against takeover and invasion. Their Umbraships scour Nodes, assault Horizon Realms and battle the "aliens" outside the Horizon and inside the Web. The Convention's

real agenda, however, is "to boldly go where no one has gone before." Ascension, to them, is to leave this decaying Earth and join the secrets of the stars. This makes them the Technocracy's loosest cannon — and the Nephandi's favorite target.

The Nephandi

These corrupters should remain shadows on the wall of your **Mage** chronicle. They are not simply "bad mages," but sworn destroyers who have been reborn to follow the Path of Descent. Any mage can commit evil deeds; the Nephandi pursue a morality of decay.

Evil as they are, the Nephandi are not stooges. Some Nephandi are maniacs, while others are subtle and conniving. All of them have reasons behind their obscenities; each has made a conscious choice to enter the Caul and undergo a dark Rebirth. Their corruption has a sound base — To have light, one must first have darkness. If that light is to survive, it must overpower darkness or be consumed. Whether or not the vision is true, most Nephandi see themselves as the beginning, the end and the beginning *of* the end. The world seems to agree with their nihilistic viewpoint; indeed, the Nephandi may actually be the strongest faction of them all.

Most Technocrats and Council mages believe the Nephandi to be banished to the outer darkness. They are wrong — far more *barabbi* exist than either faction wants to admit. The extent of their influence over Sleepers is for you to decide, but in any case, they feed on Gothic-punk despair. They rarely go about openly, but subvert and infiltrate other groups, bringing them down from within. Mood and atmosphere are important tools if the Nephandi show up.

Nephandi do not work well with others. There are rumored to be divisions among the Fallen that spark wars within their own ranks. Some are said to worship the Outsiders, while others win their gifts from astral demon hordes. Still others breed fomori in service to the primal Wyrm. Any or all of these rumors might be true. Few outsiders ever find out. The reality should be left to the players' imaginations.

The Marauders

All Marauders are insane, and madness is their calling card. No matter how sane one might appear, each Marauder harbors dangerous delusions which feed into his understanding of the dynamic core of the universe.

This madness varies from mage to mage. Some appear no more than mildly eccentric, even amusing, while others could eat toxic waste without gagging and kill children with glee. Ascension, for the Mad Ones, is as unpredictable as madness itself. For all their Wyldness, however, Marauders are still human beings — albeit humans gone forever insane through a direct line with infinite chaos. This makes them all the more frightening.

Marauders should never seem predictable. Storytellers are advised to go with their wildest instincts while keeping that human core in mind.

Sexual Politics

Sexuality is an inescapable part of the human experience, and the Awakened are not immune to its influence. As the **Mage** introduction says, anyone can be a mage; neither gender nor sexual orientation play a part. Sadly, it would be naive to assume that every group reacts with total egalitarianism. Like the agendas above, the stereotypes below are generalizations only. Every person is unique.

The Traditions, as always, stand for diversity. Some groups, like the Order of Hermes and Sons of Ether, are notably conservative. Although women, gays and bisexuals reside within these Traditions, internal dissension about "policy" is common. Others, like the Verbena and Cult of Ecstasy, are openly gynocentric and display little regard for a person's orientation. Most groups fall into middle grounds. Despite their name, few Akashic Brothers make distinctions along sexual lines — all people are considered "brothers." The Chorus, too, has largely transcended the "limitations" of its mortal prejudices. Dreamspeakers, Euthanatos and Virtual Adepts are a mixed bag; some members come from very conservative (or male-dominated) cultures and carry appropriate views, while others view women and gays as equals. The Hollow Ones, as usual, don't give a shit.

The Technocracy is notoriously chauvinistic; every person has their place, regardless of gender or preference, but the glass ceiling lives. Most ranking Technocrats view total acceptance of alternative lifestyles as counterproductive, and provide places for women who know theirs. Anyone can achieve high status in the Union's ranks, but only the Void Engineers and Progenitors seem completely blind to gender roles.

The archetypal Nephandus is a woman, though this probably has more to do with the witch-harlot stereotype than with real membership or power. As the most powerful (and fearful) human urge, sexuality has infinite possibilities for corruption. The Fallen seem to know all of them well; both genders are renowned for violence, temptations and perversions. Some Fallen Ones, it is said, are neither male nor female, but both or even genderless, thanks to magickal mutations. In any case, the faction doesn't seem to discriminate much — anyone is fair game.

Each Marauder is unique, wrapped in a cocoon of his or her own madness. The ways they deal with others of any sort or gender are as varied as they are capricious.

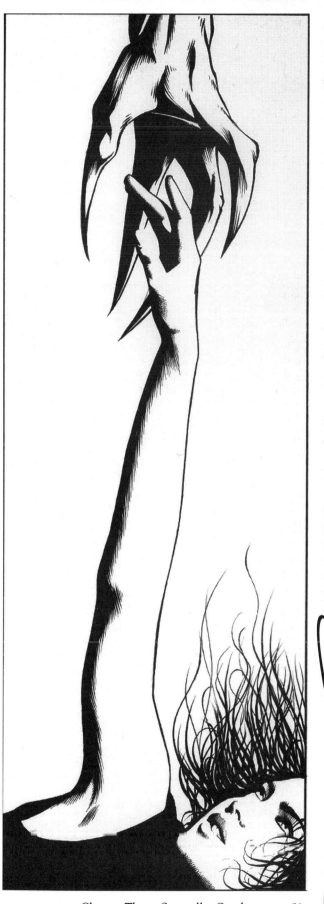

Umbral Ships

Between the worlds, beyond the Horizon, lies an endless void. In material reality, this space is airless and barren. Those few who have escaped the great barriers, however, speak of the Etherspace, or Deep Universe. Some mages traverse this space with specially-made Umbraships, rare vehicles which harness advanced Arts or technomagicks to escape Earth's physical and metaphysical gravity. Only Void Engineers and Sons of Ether, for the most part, own or design such ships. Any lucky mage, however, may find himself aboard one.

Most Umbral ships are built in the material world and "phased" through the Gauntlet with powerful Spirit and Prime magicks. This vulgar process has destroyed more than its share of voyagers, so such ships are often kept on the far side of the barrier, usually "docked" in a Horizon Realm until they're needed. Both Sons and Engineers employ "phase chambers" (known by a variety of names) to bring the ship crews across. Umbraships are invisible to the material eye, although mystick Awareness can sense their passage. Because of the expense, time and expertise required to build them, Umbraships are hard to come by. Many Awakened consider them a fanciful myth.

The most infamous of these Umbral ships, the Technocracy's Qui La Machinæ, operate within the Horizon's boundaries. Invisible to the mortal eye, they wreak havoc upon magickal places. Through elaborate navigation procedures, they shuttle throughout the Penumbra "sanitizing" mystickal Nodes into more mundane functions. These are the battleships of the Ascension War, heavily armed and armored with the technomagickal alloy Primium. Qui La Machinæ come in two different classes: X156 cruisers, employed for common sanitation, and X200 warships (called "Vaders" by overly imaginative Engineers), which are called out in the most dire of circumstances. Both types have extensive Force weaponry, Prime-fueled Quintessence draws, phase capability and a compliment of Boarder Corps troops. Both have been designed to strike fear into mage and Umbrood alike; bristling with guns and blades, they resemble floating Art Deco fortresses. The Engineers don't have many of these ships (exact numbers are classified), but the ships' fear potential makes up for their small numbers.

The Sons of Ether are more individual. Many mad scientists create Umbral jump-suits, orbital chambers, astrospheres, galactic carracks and a host of smaller ships to navigate the Etherspace and Umbral Worlds. The bewildering array of devices aboard these ships testifies to the heights of vision — and disorganization — to which starfaring Ethernauts ascend. Some have life-support systems (based on the idea that the Umbra is poisonous) and particle-beam weaponry; others have plush Victorian quarters (like the famous Victoria Station Chantry orbiting the moon), harpoons, elaborate rigging and sails, sleek designs worthy of a *Star Wars* movie or awkwardly elegant fins, domes, stabilizers, etc. For the Ethernauts, form and function are one; each ship bears the stamp of its creators.

Along the Umbral Horizon front, a series of Void Engineer satellites keeps watch for Nephandi creeping in and Ethernauts flying out. Deep Universe Research Collectives journey far into the Etherspace, ferrying curious Engineers (and often-terrified members of other Conventions) to the furthest reaches of explored space. The Engineers usually wear elaborate life-support gear, and are puzzled when they encounter other explorers without any sort of protection at all.

The Mad Ones and Nephandi, however, are the truest masters of the endless void. Marauders often float through space wrapped in their own madness, or ride bizarre beasts and ornate starships between the Shard Realms. When their war-parties cross over thin points in the Horizon, these strange invaders lay siege to any Horizon Realm they can reach (the once-great Construct Null-B has been decimated by such raids, as have other lesser-known Chantries). Ethernauts claim that the Flying Dutchman itself appears occasionally in the Deep Umbra, helmed by enigmatic madmen.

From their nightmare Realms outside the barrier, the Fallen Ones launch living Umbraships in an effort to pierce Earth's Horizon. These Nephandi warlords harness arcane powers to survive the reaches of Etherspace. Some ride monsters that shatter sanity like eggshells, while others construct semi-organic warships crewed by abominations. Fortunately, direct assaults are rare; the Fallen do not have the numbers yet to mount a truly impressive assault. Travelers into the void, however, risk their lives and souls should they encounter a Nephandus' battleship.

The most horrible Umbraships, however, are the prison spheres of Null-B. Rebellious Technomancers have been sealed, from time to time, in solitary-confinement spheres which are then sent off into infinity. The fate of eternal confinement and loneliness is worse than any execution the ruling Triumvirate could devise. Ethernauts occasionally pick up such spheres on their journeys. The inhabitants have been, without exception, quite mad.

Chapter Four: Handouts

Preston's guest sniffed at the proffered tea and clacked his cane on the stone floor.

"I come at your urgent invitation, and you offer me iced tea? Oh please!"

"It's summer in New Orleans," replied Preston calmly. "But I can provide some Earl Grey, I think. In a moment. Sit if you like."

The guest sat and adjusted the folds of his paisley silk smoking jacket, absently stroking his long, furry ears. "I say, what's this all about then? Why have you called on me?"

Preston took a deep breath. "I would like some information. I seek a Realm I've seen in my dreams, closed behind a gate of iron and a garland of lost souls. Do you know of such a place?"

The guest diddled with his lace jabot. "Perhaps I do, perhaps."

"And what do you want in exchange for this knowledge?" asked Preston.

"Not so very much," replied the guest after a thoughtful pause. "Shall we say the mantle of a Master from House Bonisagus? Or really, one from any Master in Doissetep would do quite nicely." The guest smiled. "So… did you say Earl Grey or Darjeeling, my good man?"

We've included the following handouts to make life easier for both players and Storytellers. These Sphere reference sheets may be photocopied and stuck in a folder to check what your character can do; if he had Entropy, Prime and Time, for instance, you'd copy and keep those sheets. Although the details of each Sphere must be checked in the main rulebook, these quick summations can save both time and wear and tear on the binding.

One note: Some Spheres have been expanded or revised in second edition **Mage**. These sheets reflect those changes. Players still using first edition rules with them are bound to be confused.

Correspondence

Specialties: Conjuration, Scrying, Warding, Teleportation

Correspondence involves an understanding of locations, spatial relativity and the interrelation between people and objects. This allows mages to teleport, pull rabbits out of hats, create magickal barriers and levitate or fly through the air. Correspondence is also commonly mixed with other Spheres to allow mages to work magick on subjects hundreds of miles away.

Since Correspondence deals with space and relationships, its range differs from the other eight Spheres. The theory popular among the Virtual Adepts, the most recent Masters of Correspondence, is that space is ultimately an illusion. More traditional mages explain Correspondence by the ancient doctrine of contagion: "Once together, always together." In other words, it is simpler to perform any working when there is a connection — physical, mental or spiritual — between them.

While most mages need to touch their subject to work their Arts, those skilled in Correspondence may skirt barriers or distance by forming links through space or related objects. The chart shows the successes needed to forge a link between two points. The weaker the connection, the more successes the spell requires.

• Immediate Spatial Perceptions

At this stage, the mage can intuitively estimate distances between objects, find true north (or any other direction) and sense things in her immediate vicinity without using the normal five senses. This new sense also allows her to also detect spatial instabilities, warps and wormholes.

•• Sense/Touch Space

The mage may now extend any of her five senses across intervening space. Such magickal perceptions thin the barriers between the two points in space, however, creating a weakness in the Tapestry (like those a rank one Effect can spot). Luckily, she can also re-work the fabric of space, reinforcing the Tapestry and creating a barrier to hinder scrying or the opening of actual rifts. This works like countermagick, deducting successes for each success.

In conjunction with Life or Matter, the mage may also grasp small items — house cat-sized or smaller — and pull them through the Tapestry, conjuring them from "nowhere."

••• Pierce Space/Seal Gate/Co-locality Perception

The mage may now tear a hole through space, big enough to pass through but not large enough to carry large items into. She may also seal such rifts or prevent them from opening; the greater the rift, the more difficult the feat.

She also learns to sense multiple locations at once, perceiving the various scenes as several ghostly landscapes overlapping one another. Working with the other Spheres, a mage may also grasp items governed by the Pattern Magicks and slide them through space, performing levitation and telekinesis.

•••• Rend Space/Co-locate Self

The Adept may now transport other beings and large objects. With enough successes (10+), she may even force the rent wide enough to make a permanent Gateway.

The mage may now manifest physically in multiple locations at once, though she should also use Mind 1 if she wants to think effectively in all of them, and Life 2 if she wants her multiple selves to perform separate actions.

••••• Mutate Localities/Co-location

A Master of Correspondence learns how to distort space. She can affect distances and sizes around her, stretching them and shrinking them to fit her needs. In scientific terms, the mass of objects cannot be changed, but their volumes and dimensions are like potter's clay.

She may also stack locations on top of one another in a bizarre landscape of multiple forms or connect a variety of items together. At this point, the Master's perceptions are so wildly expanded that her mundane Perception may be enhanced beyond the normal human maximum.

Entropy

Specialties: Fate, Fortune, Order, Chaos

The practical applications of Entropy are manifold. Disciples learn to quantify probability energy, which most mages call Destiny, Fate or Fortune. Through observation, a mage may spot "accidents waiting to happen" and take advantage of them, while at higher levels, the mage learns to manipulate the actual threads of probability.

Mages who study Entropy tend to specialize either in sowing chaos and confusion or in reaffirming order and reason, though some follow an enigmatic middle ground. Curses and blessings are their specialty, and they can bring the strange force of Wyrd to bear on objects, individuals and even ideas and concepts. These mages understand how all patterns break down, and thus, how they work in the first place.

Direct Entropy Effects do no damage until the fourth level, after which they do one success less than usual. Applications of entropy — crumbling walls, disintegrated bridges, etc. — are more effective, and inflict the usual damage.

• Sense Fate & Fortune

Disciples of Entropy learn to examine each thing and discern its strengths and weaknesses, examining what it is and what it does. Given this knowledge, the mage can pick a lucky horse, sense if a lock has some defect or choose the original between two identical items. Fate, however, is a fickle thing, and Fortune even more so. These insights are not perfect, just advanced.

•• Control Probability

Now that the threads of Fate have been identified, the dominos of Fortune may be pushed. Disciples learn control over probability by studying where it concentrates. This gives the mage amazing, yet subtle control over hundreds of small events. He may determine the outcome of any minor event that would normally be random. Once he discerns which apparently random events are in fact predetermined, he can then manipulate other eventualities to his own ends.

There's a limit to this control; the greater the probability he tries to affect, the more difficult the act becomes. Determining a coin-toss is simple magick. Determining the toss of the same coin 100 times in succession becomes correspondingly more difficult.

••• Affect Predictable Patterns

Machines are especially susceptible to entropy. Clocks wind down, engines break, and all things eventually decay. A Disciple of Entropy can "fix" this deterioration, causing a new television set to blow a fuse while an old junker car still runs years after it should have fallen apart. This works best on complex machines — simple objects are harder to erode or maintain this way.

A mystick at this level can also control the fate of objects or people, though his influence is still limited by the realm of possibility. The more unlikely a feat, the more difficult it becomes.

•••• Affect Life

Adepts of Entropy study how life forms begin, mature, wither, and die. Through this, a mage learns how to influence the random factors of life, giving him immense power either to destroy it or affect its development. With this magick, a mage can weave a potent spell over a living being, blessing or cursing him and his line. Other Spheres may be woven into such a charm, creating hereditary magickal gifts or flamboyant curses. These Arts affect probability, not Life Patterns themselves.

••••• Affect Thought

Masters of Entropy expand their control over reality by studying the ways in which ideas change over time. Thoughts, they point out, can be molded, shaped and influenced over time. While the Masters of Mind rudely subjugate the minds of others, Masters of Entropy merely point out things that will strike a person a particular way and let his thoughts follow the natural progression to other possibilities.

Master of Entropy who specialize in chaos can confuse a person simply by making a few weird comments, while those specializing in order can present logical arguments to guide that person's ideas to some higher (or at least different) conclusion. Masters who specialize in Fate or Fortune can lead subjects to inescapable conclusions or spark random, creative thoughts, which a subject may absorb as he sees fit. This may lead to paradigm shifts, new faiths or insanity.

Forces

Specialties: Elements (any or all), Technology, Physics, Weather

Mages who understand the Sphere of Forces know that there is much that "civilization" does not understand about the elements. Masters of this Pattern Art can manipulate and create natural forces as she pleases.

Mages who want to cause serious damage often study this Sphere. An Effect utilizing Forces adds one additional success to damage rolls. Certain energies are limited by Sphere levels; simple manifestations can be used at lower levels, while massive phenomena are limited to the higher ranks. Most larger Effects also require plenty of successes. Other mages tend to give Masters of Forces some distance, as they are infamously Paradox-prone and their magick tends to be very messy.

• Perceive Forces

The mage can perceive all types of energy flows, sensing wavelengths far beyond the limited range of visible light and sonic frequencies upon which normal mortals rely. She may see anything from infrared light to x-rays to gravity waves.

•• Control Minor Forces

All the positive forces are essentially the same — sound, light, heat, etc. — as are the negative forces — silence, darkness, cold and so on. While a mage at this level of understanding cannot fundamentally change either positive or negative energies, she can exercise some degree of control over their ebb and flow. Sound and silence may be sent in different directions, light and darkness may be bent, focused and diffused to change apparent colors, displace a mage's image, wrap her in shadows, or focus a flashlight into a fine laser.

The amount of energy that can be controlled at this level is limited; the mage could short circuit a house, but not an apartment building. The larger the force to be controlled, and the degree of that control, the more successes the spell demands. A candle flame can be made to flare with only one success, but a bonfire requires five or more. To control greater forces requires Forces 4.

••• Transmute Minor Forces

The mage can now change one force into another, flip positive into negative, or create or destroy forces as she likes, summoning them out of thin air and dissolving them into same. With this level of Forces alone, a mage may change one force into another. Radiation may be transformed into sound, heat into cold or light into darkness. With a conjunctional Effect involving Matter or Life, a mage may transmute things of those Spheres into a Force of the strength governed by this level.

Alternately, the mage may turn Quintessence into one of the baser forces or transform base energy into pure ether, transmuting the elements or summoning forces from "nowhere." With enough successes, a mage with this power can now freeze enemies solid or incinerate them on the spot, blow up cars or fly through the air. With Life 4, she may even transform herself into a being of living fire, a shadow or a chill.

•••• Control Major Forces

This power works like Forces 2 above, but the maximum for that level is the minimum for this one. With enough successes, she may focus the light of the sun into a laser canon, redirect missiles mid-flight, or melt glaciers while lakes are frozen solid. Most such Effects, of course, are quite vulgar.

••••• Transmute Major Forces

This level operates like Forces 3 above, but with enough successes, the degree of power a mage may access is almost limitless. Large Effects require many successes, as well as logic — it's easier to brew a storm during monsoon season than in the middle of a drought, for example — but a Master of Forces may conjure hurricanes, firestorms, tidal waves, earthquakes and nuclear blasts.

Life

Specialties: Shapeshifting, Disease/ Healing, Improvement, Cloning/ Creation

Mages of Life are invaluable to a Chantry; their powers may heal both normal and aggravated wounds, and can cause the same. Damage from the Sphere of Life is fairly standard, but sorcerers who know this Art need not simply kill opponents. They may also improve their bodies (or others'), sometimes transforming them into new creatures altogether.

Transformation or mutation works the same way as it does with any other Sphere; to change one thing into another (or create it from "nowhere"), the mystick must use another Sphere to do it.

Generally speaking, the Sphere of Life governs items still containing living cells, even if the item is technically dead. If something is alive enough to be planted in the ground to sprout, or is still serviceable for transplant surgery or at least tissue cultures, Life rules it.

• Sense Life

By reading Life Patterns, a mage can learn a lot about a life form — its age, its sex and every aspect of its health — and can also sense different forms of life nearby.

•• Alter Simple Patterns/Heal Self

This rank's magicks can alter the structure of basic life forms, from microscopic viruses and bacteria to creatures as complex as insects and shellfish. He can heal simple creatures or kill them, cause crabs to sprout extra legs, trees to bear fruit or bees to release the pheromones which signal a swarm. Whatever he does, the creatures themselves remain what they always were — he can mutate them, but cannot transform them.

The mage may also correct (or create) breaks in his own Pattern, to heal or harm himself as he desires.

••• Alter Self/Heal Life/Transform-Create Simple Patterns

At this rank, the mage can alter his own Pattern, making subtle improvements and variations as he did with simple Patterns at Life 2. He cannot substantially change what he is (a human), but can change his gender or appearance or physically modify his body to grow claws, fur, gills, etc.

Simple Patterns are now his to command; he may turn them inside-out, change one into another or even create them entirely from other Patterns, through conjunctional Effects. Unfortunately, any life form he creates has no mind beyond what it held before. The mystick may also heal (or harm) other people as he did himself at the previous rank.

•••• Alter Complex Life Patterns/Transform Self

A mage who reaches this rank can change the structure of any complex Life Patterns, including those of other sentient beings. As with Life 2, the creatures subjected to this magick still retain their original form, but radical variations on that basic form are still possible.

A Life Adept can alter her form to resemble another living being of approximately the same size and mass. She may become a deer, but not a mouse. Special abilities — water breathing, flight, etc. — do not carry over at this level without additional Life Effects, and moving around in the new form will take getting used to.

••••• Transform-Create Complex Life Patterns/Perfect Metamorphosis

A Master of Life can transform others as she transformed herself at the previous rank. At this level, she can attain any form she desires and alter others the same way.

This carries its own problems. A higher being transformed into a lower one tends to trade intelligence for survival instincts, while a lower life form changed into a higher one has similar problems. The perfect self-metamorphosis a Master achieves, however, has no such problems. A mage who shapeshifts at this level carries her mind and Arts with her. Whatever she becomes, that form is as natural as the one she was born into.

At this level, the mage can weave a new Pattern to create any life form, even a human body, using conjunctional magick to translate it from energy, matter or pure Quintessence with the appropriate rank of Forces, Matter or Prime. Unfortunately, the life form created has no mind or soul beyond the base material or the Resonance it carries.

Matter

Specialties: Transmutation, Shaping, Conjuration, Complex Patterns

This Sphere concerns itself with non-living matter; the precise line between this Sphere and the Sphere of Life, like the precise line between the Elements, varies from Tradition to Tradition. In general, assume that a subject that contains living or nearly-living tissue (blood, for instance) falls under Life, whereas dead simple tissue (hair) falls under Matter.

Wherever the division lies, students of Matter first learn to analyze their subject, then to transmute one basic substance into another. After this, a mage learns to rework the shapes of items, craft articles of great complexity and finally create items of wonder and the substances of legend.

• Matter Perceptions

The Disciple of Matter begins by recognizing the various Patterns of Matter, including the underlying structures that give objects their shapes and physical properties. This allows her to detect things hidden from normal senses. In addition to sensing the composition and properties of Matter, the Disciple can discern structures hidden within structures; material no longer forms a barrier to her senses.

•• Basic Transmutation

The mage may transmute one substance into another, without changing its shape, temperature or basic state (solid, liquid, gas). Mages of mystick Traditions can change milk into cream or mahogany into oak, while scientists change water to acid or lead into gold. The more radical the transmutation, the more successes the spell requires. It's easier to change water into wine (one success) than into sulfuric acid (three), and more complicated to turn stones into bread (three successes) than sourdough into rye (one).

A mage may also use conjunctional Effects involving other Pattern Spheres to briefly transform items governed by Forces, Life or Prime into basic Patterns of Matter, including changing living beings into stone (Life 4/ Matter 2) or spinning moonlight into thread (Forces 3/ Matter 2). With Prime 2, she may harness the ether to create (or uncreate) any *simple, basic* thing composed of *one common homogeneous substance*. A granite boulder shaped vaguely like a woman is possible, but a dainty china shepherdess is not. A bowlful of oatmeal or even blueberry pancakes could be made to appear, but not a baroque wedding cake. The more rare and/or complex a given substance, the more difficult it is to create — it's easier to create glass than diamonds.

••• Alter Form

At the third rank of Matter, the mage can change the shape of inanimate objects however she desires, or temporarily alter their state to make solids become liquids or liquids become gas. Permanent changes in state require Rank 5. A mage who understands this rank may sculpt matter into any shape she pleases, limited only by the physical properties of the materials she uses. Broken items may also be repaired seamlessly, if she has the mundane knowledge to do so.

•••• Complex Transmutation

Adepts of Matter may now perform radical changes to physical materials and craft complex items involving several common substances or one or two rare ones. Any sort of regular matter may be changed into any other — a squirt pistol into a loaded zipgun (three successes) or a trash dumpster into a small tank (five successes). The more radical the transformation, the more difficult the feat.

With conjunctional Effects, the Patterns of Life, Forces or Prime itself may be transmuted into complex Matter, allowing mages to turn pumpkins into gilded coaches, lightning bolts into swords or the Quintessential ether into master keys. Complex organic creations are also possible, including silk ballgowns, roast chickens and Persian rugs.

••••• Alter Properties

At this pinnacle of understanding, Masters of Matter may create substances which do not exist in nature by taking existing materials and altering their physical properties, or even make one object immaterial to some other substance. All the substances of legends and comic books are possible with this level of magick. Masters build castles with paper-thin walls and wear armor that feels like silk and weigh less than a feather. The rare prizes of Technocratic science, such as the manmade radioactive elements, are also reserved for this level.

Mind

Specialties: Communication, Illusion, Self-Empowerment, Astral Travel

Masters of Mind have opened their mental faculties far beyond mortal scope. Perception, communication, even domination are their province. Mind Arts pack little physical punch — they do one successes less on the Damage chart — but have endless subtle applications. Most Effects, cleverly cast and helped along with Social rolls, can be used coincidentally.

• Sense Thoughts & Emotions/Empower Self

The mage begins to sense the thoughts and emotions around her. Though she cannot read them, she can sense their strength and intensity. A mystick may also read the psychic impressions left on objects. At this stage, she cannot read any actual thoughts or images, but can sense "good" or "bad vibes" from an object or place.

The Mind initiate also learns to influence her dreams and shield herself from others' thoughts and emotions. With work (a magick roll), she can hide her aura and shield her thoughts from casual observation — though determined and perceptive mages and other beings may still be able to read them.

•• Read Surface Thoughts/Create Impressions/ Mental Impulse

The mage learns how to read memories "attached" to objects by others' minds (basic psychometry) and scan surface thoughts from unshielded minds. The greater the emotional content, the easier it is to read. She can also leave psychic impressions on objects or places intentionally, too, and can send them out until they find their target. Complex thoughts cannot be transmitted this way, but single words, images or emotional impulses can.

This level also allows her to create more elaborate shields in her mind and control her dreams to some extent. Two mages of this same rank can also form a primitive mental link by dropping their shields and reading each other's conscious minds.

••• Mental Link/ Walk Among Dreams

The mage can now establish a clear link between her own consciousness and the minds of others. She can use this link for telepathic communications — or invasions. At this rank, the mage has full command of perceptual illusions or psychic disturbances. These psychic assaults take many forms, but their end goal is to turn the victim into a mental vegetable.

The mage may now contact the minds of other dreamers in her sleep and begin to explore the Dream Realms. While waking, she may also use her abilities to enter the dreaming consciousness of others, though such trips are risky.

•••• Control Conscious Mind/Walk Among Dreams

A Mind Adept can actually take over another person's mind and occupy his body for her own ends. Once this invasion has begun, she may control her victim directly, cure or cause insanity, change his memories or set up posthypnotic suggestions. The mage can overlay her subject's aura with another of a completely different color and pattern. The victim may slowly recover as the subconscious mind reasserts the true memories, but the subject's Demeanor is usually irrevocably altered.

The Adept can also leave her dreams behind and make brief excursions into the astral reaches. These trips must be short and can become dangerous. For each success the mystick rolls, she may leave her meditating body for one turn. Afterward, she returns to her physical self.

••••• Control Subconscious/Untether/ Forge Psyche

A Master of Mind rules not only his own mind, but other minds as well. He may completely rewrite someone's personality until his thoughts (and Nature Trait) bear no resemblance to anything that existed before.

The mage may also divorce a psyche from the body, switch minds between subjects and merge, copy or transfer the entire sum of a person's memories and knowledge from one body to another. His powers allow him to increase a subject's intelligence and wits to genius levels (5 dots) and may begin to increase his own beyond that. Complete astral travel becomes possible now; a Master of Mind can leave her body for hours or even days at a time.

The greatest power of a Master of Mind, however, is the ability to create true conscious thought. A Master may create another thinking, rational mind where none existed before, expanding its intelligence and designing its personality however she likes.

Prime

Specialties: Channeling, Perceptions, Filling Patterns, Draining Patterns

Prime is the study of Quintessence, the raw stuff of True Magick. It exists everywhere, and all things are composed of it, though some sources are easier to work than others. The most accessible forms of raw magick are the Quintessence stored in a mage's Avatar or crystallized into Tass. More dangerous to use, but no less possible, is the Quintessence which sustains the Life Patterns. The most difficult form of all to use is the Quintessence which forms the Patterns of creation, though a Master of Prime may tap this source as well.

Prime is essential when conjuring things from pure thought into existence, or when sustaining things which run from a magickal source (like Talismans). Bringing Patterns of Life, Matter or Forces into being "from nothing" demands Prime 2, while "recharging" magickal energies requires Prime 3.

• Etheric Senses

A mage can sense basic Quintessential energy — the Nodes where it collects or wells up, the Tass in which it crystallizes, and the Quintessential ebbs and flows which mark the times of greatest magick. He may also notice creatures and objects charged with magickal energy. Such perceptions vary from mage to mage. Without the first rank of Prime, the mage cannot store free Quintessence within his own Pattern beyond the amount he receives from his Avatar. Mages without Prime magicks cannot gain Quintessence ratings above their Avatar Background Trait.

•• Weave Odyllic Force/ Fuel Pattern

The mage attains some control over the shifting Quintessential energy, and can divert small streams to flow differently or reweave them. When he conceives of an object, it takes on some degree of solidity. By channeling Prime Force through his concept, the sorcerer can transform it into a physical form.

••• Channel Quintessence

At rare sites (Nodes) and on rare days (Junctures), Quintessential Force focuses into Primal energy. The resulting flow is called "free" Quintessence. Another Prime aspect, "raw" Quintessence, makes up Patterns, flows through living beings and coalesces in the tremendous pool of Quintessence from which mages draw the energies for Pattern magick. At this rank, a mystick understands how to draw these "surplus" energies out of their Patterns and channel them into new ones.

•••• Expel Base Energy

While Disciples of Prime are largely limited to detecting and manipulating free Quintessence, Adepts of Prime learn to channel raw Quintessence. They can pull Quintessence out of the Patterns of matter and energy, affecting a Pattern's substance in reality. Each shard of inanimate matter and each spark of energy has Quintessence stored within. Adepts can expel the Quintessence from these Patterns, recycling it into the cosmic pool of raw Quintessence. Without Quintessence in its Pattern, that matter or energy ceases to exist.

Adepts who know enough about Matter or Forces can use conjunctional Effects to alter the amount of Quintessence stored in various parts of these Patterns, thereby "dissolving" different aspects or properties of the energy or matter. A sorcerer could make solids become insubstantial, cause a magnet to have only one pole, remove a chemical's ability to form nuclear bonds with other chemicals (this process would, for example, make an acid unable to corrode), or cause objects to lose their mass yet remain solid. While Pattern magicks alone can do the same thing, extracting a target's raw Quintessence is a direct and "easy" way to alter it.

••••• Alter Flow

Masters of Prime delve into truly advanced theories. Such Masters can alter established flows of raw Quintessence — those flowing through Life Patterns. Living beings interact with Quintessence in a unique manner. Their Quintessence is not stored in their Patterns, but runs continuously through them. By damming this flow, the mage can extinguish the spark of life within the creature.

Masters can also *increase* the flow of Quintessence through a Pattern. This means nothing to life forms without strong Avatars, but Awakened ones can instantly recharge their Avatars' Quintessence.

Spirit

Specialties: Dimensional Science, Spirit Dealings, Umbral Travel, Possessions

No other Sphere, perhaps, marks the line between mystick and Technomancer as clearly as Spirit; some regard the Otherworlds as the base of the mortal world, while others consider them just another frontier. This Sphere encompass skills for traveling through the Otherworlds, dealing with spirits and surviving alien environments like the Deep Umbra. While the game systems do not distinguish shamanism from spirit-tech, the foci, styles and intents vary a lot.

Unlike most Spheres, Spirit magicks often use the local Gauntlet rating (see screen chart) as a difficulty. The thicker the barrier, the harder it is to penetrate, and vice versa. Any Spirit Effect, therefore, that passes between the material world and the Otherworlds uses the Gauntlet as its difficulty. Vulgar and coincidental Effects still incur the usual amounts of Paradox, however.

• Spirit Sight/ Spirit Sense

The Spirit initiate gains the ability to sense the Near Umbra around her, allowing her to see auras, ghosts and spirits. Using such insight can be dangerous; mysticks attuned to the spiritual world often miss things in the physical one. She can also "read" the strength of the local Gauntlet and sense an item containing spirit essence.

•• Touch Spirit/ Manipulate Gauntlet

The mage now gains the ability to briefly touch spirits and objects in the Penumbra — she can push a spirit out of a room or hit one over the head. Although this magick allows only brief contact (a turn or two), it can be enough. She can also speak through the Gauntlet, or extend her perceptions to **Plumb the Deep Umbra** and detect the fringes of eternity.

A mystick can also thin (or strengthen) the local Gauntlet. Each success lowers or raises the Gauntlet difficulty by -/+ 1 for one turn; three successes would affect that difficulty by 3 for three turns. Naturally, this roll must first succeed against the original Gauntlet rating. The Gauntlet cannot be brought lower than difficulty 4.

••• Pierce Gauntlet/ Rouse & Lull Spirit

A mage may now make a hole in the Gauntlet and "step sideways" into the Umbra. Her body and possessions become ephemera, the stuff of spirit; as things of the material world, however, they carry an odd glow. Any action the mystick takes against an Umbrood creature now will be felt. Possessions are difficult to transform; entering skyclad (nude) requires only the usual successes at the usual difficulty. Normal clothing and items add +1 to both difficulty and successes needed. Bulky gear demands a +2 increase. The mage cannot bring through anything she could not normally carry.

With conjunctional Matter 3 and Prime 2 Arts, the mystick may create short-lived items out of ephemera. These creations must be built as if they were material items, and fade away when the Effect's duration ends.

The mage also gains the power to rouse or lull spirits. Rousing is like calling, simply louder, while lulling puts an Umbrood into brief slumber with a contested Willpower vs. Willpower roll. The more powerful the spirit, the more difficult it is to awaken or put back to sleep.

•••• Rend Gauntlet/ Seal Breach/ Bind Spirit

The mage may now rip the Gauntlet asunder and travel through without difficulty or repair breaches which others have made. Creating such rips is, of course, highly vulgar.

The mage may now compel spirits to appear and bind them or force them into objects, creating fetishes. The more powerful the spirit, the more successes it takes to bind them. A brave (or foolish) shaman may also channel a spirit's powers through herself. This shuts out any other magick she might do while the Umbrood possesses her, though she can access its Charms, speak with its voice and perform feats of incredible physical prowess. Many spirits can only be forced out through contested Willpower rolls (difficulty 7-10) or the reverse of this same power — exorcism.

••••• Forge Ephemera/ Outward Journeys

A Master of Spirit gains a divine power, for she may now take ephemera, the substance of Spirit, reweave it, repair it or rip it asunder. The mage may now heal spirits' Power (as per the Damage chart), help create Horizon Realms or Umbral Domains or even attack a victim's Avatar through the dreaded Gilgul rite.

The Master may also use her power to break free from the Horizon and explore the Far Realms and Deep Umbra. This magick allows her to survive the ravages of Etherspace for short periods while she speeds towards her chosen destination.

Time

Specialties: Perceptions, Conjunctional Uses, Travel, Temporal Control

Time is perhaps the hardest Art to comprehend. Mysticks who pursue it argue theory more than any other mages — especially the theories regarding time travel. The only clearly documented form of it involves skipping forward into the future. While travel into the past is theoretically possible, it remains beyond even Time Masters' grasp.

Time works well with other Spheres; by hooking Time magicks into other Effects, a mystick can prolong or trigger certain spells. Most Time Effects are highly vulgar; only time perceptions and triggers can remain unnoticed for long. Time perceptions enable a mystick to search the future or past for some hidden secret. When scrying forward or backward in time this way, the number of successes scored on the magickal Effect roll determines how far into the past the Time mage can perceive. Durations for other Time Effects are determined normally.

• Time Sense

The mage develops a precise internal clock, and can detect certain time-based phenomena, sensing the approach of such disturbances and "feeling" where in dimensional space the phenomena will appear. At this level, mages may also detect temporal phenomena weaker than actual rifts, like spots where a mystick steps forward in Time, sends something forward, or scrys into the future or past.

•• Past/Future Sight

The mage can now shift her perceptions forward or backward in time. Those who do so often experience flashes of pre-or-postcognition. Reading the past requires more successes to perform, but its results are fairly certain. Precognition is less difficult, but the futures foreseen — especially far futures — tend to be inaccurate. By itself, this Effect allows a mage to scry in her current location. With Correspondence 2, she may scry out any time and any place in the world, while Entropy 2 lets her view several possible futures and pick the most probable one.

Some mages reverse this magick and thicken the walls of time, making other Time Effects more difficult. Each success a mage gets on this sort of magick subtracts from a future (or past) success of some other mage to spy on the mage's present doings.

••• Time Contraction/ Dilation

The mage can now accelerate or slow time as she desires. Mysticks often describe these Effects as "contracting" or "dilating" time. While these moments seem to pass normally to an observer, he sees more things happen during that time than would normally be possible. A mage using such Effects can take one additional action for every success over the second.

•••• Time Determinism

The mage can now cause absolute shifts in time, taking a field of time and freezing it; a falling arrow may be stopped mid-flight or a man placed in a state of suspended animation. This is a powerful Effect when used in conjunction with other magicks, as the mage can choose the moment which "triggers" a magickal time bomb. Such "hanging" Effects are the type of time-based phenomenon that mages with **Time Sense** can detect. Other magickal Effects can be worked into the temporal program so long as that Effect, and its trigger, are set in advance.

••••• Future Travel/ Time Immunity

A Time Master can shift objects through time, plucking something out of the flow of time and repositioning it at some other point. The new position could be seconds or centuries away from the field's original place in time. Such Effects are firmly linked to their point of origin; ripples exist where they once were until their reappearance. This forms a continuous thread which the Master can pull at any time he sees fit. Such Arts are obviously vulgar, and any Disciple of Time can recognize an anchored time Effect and gauge the time when it will come due.

Masters can also immunize themselves from time. During this "time" outside of Time, a mage perceives the world as a collection of still images that he may manipulate as he pleases. As a conjunctional Effect with Life or Matter, he may take other creatures and objects "out of time" as well.